Sustainable Me II

COUNTERINTUITIVE CONSERVATISM

By Ben Thomas

Ben Thomas

ISBN-10: 1492746673
ISBN-13: 978-1492746676

Original Thomas Home Bensalem Church Road, Eagle Springs, North Carolina

This is a rendering of the original home site in rural North Carolina where the author spent the first 19 years of his life. In the summer the great white oak tree provided a shady comfort during the hot and humid weather. The garden was located directly behind the house as a rule, although occasionally in the foreground. A tall pear tree is seen to the left. Further behind the house and to the left were 47 acres of fields, forests, creeks, a farm pond, pastures, barns, and other sheds. The home still stands today but has not been occupied since 1967.

Table of Contents

TABLE OF CONTENTS (CONTINUED)

Ben Thomas

Sustainable Me II
Counterintuitive Conservatism

By Ben Thomas

ACKNOWLEDGEMENTS

To my wife for embracing my "journey" and for sacrificing her time, her talents and often her best desires to stand by my side.

To my parents for providing a home of love and for teaching me how to live a sustainable life.

To my two grandfathers for surviving two World Wars and the Great Depression by the use of every sustainable means available.

To my God and Savior Jesus Christ for teaching in His Word that all of Creation is the work of His hands and shows the wonder and glory of his presence.

To the teachers, staff, students, families, s and friends of Big Oak Christian Academy fore being willing to *Reduce, Reuse,* and *Recycle* in order to teach the four R's: *Readin', 'rittin', 'Rithmetic,* and *Religion.*

To Mr. Alex Frye who helped a young couple's dream come true, helped design an earth-bermed, passive solar home and built it.

To the friends who encouraged me to write

Sustainable Me:

Tips and Terms for the Environmentally Conscious

And

Sustainable Me II: Counterintuitive Conservatism

INTRODUCTION

Sustainable Me II

ENVIRONMENTAL CONSCIOUSNESS

CONSERVATIVES TOE THE LINE

THE AUTHORS ENVIRONMENTAL JOURNEY

Why should I be eco-conscious?" you ask. There is a very simple reason: We live on one earth together. If we treat earth like a community dumping ground it becomes polluted. If we treat it well by being eco-conscious, the earth may remain a clean place, perfect for living, for ourselves and generations to come.

Being "eco-conscious" means being aware of what you are doing, buying, using, and what it does to the environment. You can find many ways to help save our environment by becoming involved with many environmental causes and green organizations. These groups also will provide many ways and opportunities to help keep our world safe and ecologically sound.

The concerns of creating a worldwide culture are not confined within the boundaries of a single nation. -"Many people believe that we are facing an ecological disaster. Every day we hear horrific statistics: the process seems unstoppable. And the destruction recognizes no national frontiers. I know all this, yet I cannot really comprehend it. I have the simple thought that my day starts differently if, in the morning, the sun is shining and I can gaze upon a tree bursting with strength. It smiles at me and all at once I feel like smiling back." Arpad Goncz, President of Hungary.

The growth and development of awareness, understanding and consciousness toward the biophysical environment and its problems, including human interactions and effects is a proper definition of eco-consciousness. Major problems towards progress in converting those less likely to support environmental causes include elitism of environmentalists, stubborn reluctance of conservatives to move "green" ideas from the political to the real world, and the unwillingness of either side to focus on a common denominator rather than the myriad of differences in ideology.

The blame game is standard. Here is a word of wisdom from actor and environmental advocate Ed Asner: -"We all moan and groan about the loss of the quality of life through the destruction of our ecology, and yet each one of us, in our own little comfortable ways, contributes daily to that destruction. It's time now to awaken in each one of us the respect and attention our beloved mother deserves."

Another problem is the adamant refusal of members of the political conservative and the Christian evangelical members of our society, for the most part, to "toe the line" when it comes to environmentalism, which is perceived to be a liberal issue. How to woo this huge demographic of conservatives and Christians to join the environmental mission is critical to its success. The idea "to toe the line" essentially refers "To conforming to an established standard or political program." So, on all sides of the political spectrum, members are hesitant to make and overture, much less a step toward conciliation to this or any other issue.

Having been born and brought up in the southern United States, it is logical that I was a conservative, evangelical, Christian Republican. So my destiny was sealed you might think. However, we were poor, we were environmentally conscious, we reused, reduced, and recycled our resources with a passion. We were evangelical environmentalists!

11

Not unlike another Republican environmentalist, Theodore Roosevelt, who remarked "Here is your country. Cherish these natural wonders, cherish the natural resources, cherish the history and romance as a sacred heritage, for your children and your children's children. Do not let selfish men or greedy interests skin your country of its beauty, its riches or its romance." Conservatives today should quit their custom and refuse in the future to allow eco-consciousness to *belong* to any one group.

The author's path to environmentalism began essentially at birth. Living in an old converted sawmill shack with my maternal grandfather, I came home from the hospital to a house off the grid save for the use of six light bulbs (one for each of the five rooms and one for the front porch. There was a water well with a windless and a bucket on a rope. And there was a path to the woods for necessary purposes. My family could only afford to purchase the basic staples that we could not produce on the farm and organics, an unfamiliar term, was a way of life for us.

How times have changed. Today it is in vogue as "organic farming" but then it was simply called survival. Refrigerator? No, we had an ice box and looked forward to the delivery of a 2x2x4 foot block of ice each week to keep fresh milk, butter, and home grown fruits and vegetables chilled. I must confess that we did own a radio by which my parents listened to sermons. Radio drama, and whatever music was acceptable for a Christian to hear.

We weren't thinking about being environmentally sound or living a sustainable lifestyle. Nonetheless, we were eco-conscious, healthy, happy, and complete in our lifestyle and our environment.

Carbon Footprint? From the '49 Ford car, to the '51 Ford pickup, to the '61 Mercury Comet—we went to town two times a month for necessities and on Sunday and Wednesday to church. It's terrifying how much "stuff" we need today in comparison.

The general lack of concern for the environment by most of society is appalling. The very rich who seem to fill themselves above any concern as well as the very poor who are uninformed, uneducated, and even unable to participate in environmental issues should also be among those who are reached with the message of being "green." They are not my focus in this book.; but I can't go another page without a reprimand to the rich and famous who live in enormous homes, nurture exotic food fads, drive high-powered cars, SUVs, and ride to and fro in limos and private planes while espousing inflated ideals of non-profit participation.

The goal of this volume is to assert the ability and responsibility for conservatives to act conservatively in every area of their lives. Family values and Christian values must include environmental values as a part of the package.

ENVIRONMENTAL ISSUES and CONFLICT RESOLUTION

Sustainable Me II

CLIMATE CHANGE

GLOBAL WARMING

DEGRADING OZONE LAYER

CHAPTER 1

"At the end of our exploring we will arrive where we started, and know the place for the first time."

— T.S. Eliot —

ENVIRONMENTAL CONSIDERATIONS

CLIMATE CHANGE

One of the biggest perceived threats to humanity and nature is climate change. The threat of climate change is real . Greenhouse gas emissions are rising more rapidly that formerly predicted and the world is warming more quickly. Humanity has released enough greenhouse gases into the atmosphere during the industrial age that now we are feeling the effects of an warmer world. Pronounced droughts, floods, wildfires, and storms are expected more frequently and rising seas will inundate coastlines. Climate patterns are beginning to change around the world due to these events.

The climate system varies naturally over a wide range of time scales. Prior to the industrial revolution change may be explained by natural causes such as changes in solar energy, volcanic eruptions and changes in greenhouse concentrations. In recent times, however, research indicates that climate change can not be explained by natural causes alone. Scarce water in certain areas prompting mass migrations, social upheaval, and wars all have their impact.

We are now seeing evidence of melting polar ice caps, catastrophic weather and threatened ecosystems which are all indicators of human influence on climate change.

Human production of greenhouse gases mainly streaming from carbon dioxide and methane are major influences on climate change. Nevertheless, despite these urgent problems there are technological developments are well as meaningful lifestyle changes that we can make to help reduce climate change.

Scientific skepticism about climate change is healthy. Scientists should always challenge themselves to improve their understanding. Yet this isn't what happens with climate change denial. Skeptics often spend time that supports man-made climate change and yet embrace any argument that purports to refute man-made change.

Conservative organizations who track climate patterns over long periods of time can easily point to warmer and wetter periods in the earth's history. To them this is proof that recent changes are simply the result of naturally occurring patterns and not to current unusually high levels of greenhouse gases that may be spiking erratic weather patterns and climate change.

U.S. Senator Sheldon Whitehouse, one of Congress's few outspoken environmental advocates, is making a new argument for legislative action on climate change: Lawmakers who oppose future measures to reverse global warming, Whitehouse argues, will pay a price — in votes. Whitehouse, who recently announced the formation of a bicameral task force to address the issue, compared climate change to social issues like gay rights and immigration reform. Even stronger rhetoric from leading Democrats such as Al Gore and Hillary Clinton is failing to garner support.

Fewer Americans view global warming as a "very serious problem" today than just year ago. If you exclude partisan Democrats who will follow President Obama on everything, you're left with about 25 percent of Americans who think that global warming is a very serious problem. Even worse for Democrats who are hoping to make real progress in the 2014 elections, the Huffington Post/YouGov poll conducted the week that Hurricane Sandy hit asked the question, "If it meant we could stop climate change, would you personally be willing to pay 50 percent more on your gas and electricity bills?" 54 percent of respondents — a clear majority — said that they would *not* be willing (including 52.5 percent of independents and 80 percent of Republicans). Only 21 percent said they would be willing to pay more. So even when using a question that leads those polled to think they could "stop climate change" once and for all, a majority of Americans still says no to paying more out of pocket to do so. It seems that those most likely to vote in the 2014 elections would be heavily against the increased costs that the Democrats favor, even for doing even less than "stopping climate change."

House Republicans have summoned the leaders of top federal agencies to a hearing to examine their plans to implement a sweeping climate change agenda that President Obama outlined in a recent speech. The LA Times chooses to describe this as a final chance, "to wrest a measure of control over the administration's climate change agenda."

Since President Obama came out with his call for "market-based legislation to reduce emissions of heat-trapping greenhouse gases" there is an opportunity to make some progress on coming together. This could be a chance to get all of the government experts to weigh in on exactly what the costs are, not only in direct federal dollars, but in jobs lost and increased prices at the pump and in taxpayers' heating and utility bills.

There is an old saying in the south, "Everybody talkin' about heaven ain't goin' there." In the case of climate change, "Everybody talking about climate change ain't been *there*." The fact of the matter is that there is even disagreement among meteorological scientists in the interpretation of data regarding climate change.

"Taken as a whole, the range of published evidence indicates that the net damage costs of climate change are likely to be significant and to increase over time.," according to the Intergovernmental Panel on Climate Change. Perhaps discussing this issue in the context of economic terms will motivate more republicans to get on board.

Both liberals and conservatives favor a greater emphasis on alternative energy sources such as wind and solar and on modifying buildings to make them more energy-efficient. Both groups reject putting more emphasis on building coal or oil-fired power plants. Still one difference is that conservatives favor more emphasis on nuclear energy, while opponents fear potential melt downs as well as long term hazards. Concern about climate change appear to be a key factor driving support for alternative energy sources and greater efficiency.

ConservAmerica was founded in 1995 to resurrect the GOP's great conservation tradition and to restore natural resource conservation and sound environmental protection as fundamental elements of the Republican Party's vision for America. Conservation is Conservative! ® is their battle cry.

George W. Bush made a series of promises to appease the moderates when he ran for president. Once the buzz surrounding his agenda subsided, we can reasonably see that these promises were not kept. Bush would cite a contrary congress for refusing him to earn the credit for these campaign promises. On the environment, Bush promised to regulate carbon dioxide emissions and to budget $100 million per year for rain forest preservation. It seems the reaction from both political parties was to follow the follow the same pattern: "Make certain the other side does not get credit."

Environmentalists exacerbated the Republican shift away from environmental issues by allying forcefully with the Democratic Party. Environmental groups gave Bush little credit for his accomplishments. When they denounced Bush for his failings, and allowed Democrats to claim the environmental mantle exclusively for themselves, environmentalists helped to drive both parties to the extremes. The Democrats veered toward warning of environmental apocalypse, while Republicans went to the other pole, denying the threat of environmental problems.

The real problem here is still care and concern for our air, and the atmosphere in general. The solution is more complicated because we will get nowhere close to solving this problem until we solve the foundational and complex problem of getting a majority of our leaders on the same page. I do not see a reason why Democrats and Republicans, liberals and conservatives, tree-huggers and the lumber industry, vegans and meat-eaters, clean energy proponents and fossil fuel advocates—why we all can't put aside our differences and concentrate on issues upon which we agree. One obvious way is to stop the name calling and finger pointing and to find any areas possible where we agree. It's a childish concept, but praise the positive steps and provide opposing views gently without an in-your-face attitude. Win them over and include them in our mutual victories without giving in to that great human need of saying "I told you so."

Yale and George Mason University recently asked American Republicans and Republican-leaning Independents about their views on energy and climate change. A large majority of respondents (77 percent) support using clean, renewable energy in the US much more (51 percent) or somewhat more (26 percent) than it is used today. Among those who support expanded use of clean energy, 69 percent feel we should be taking action *immediately*.

A slight majority (52 percent) supports using fossil fuels in the US much less (21 percent) or somewhat less (31 percent) than we do today. Among those who'd like to see less fossil fuel use, the most common preference is to do it "immediately."

Confirming the positive approach as being most effective, the terms that resonate most for describing energy types are "fossil fuel"—over terms like conventional energy or dirty energy—and "clean energy"—rather than terms like renewable or advanced. Getting our conservative friends on board should be our first goal; then they can become familiar with the vocabulary.

A majority of the respondents feel that taking steps to reduce our fossil fuel use will benefit the nation in a number of ways. The most popular benefit for this group is "freeing us from dependence on foreign oil." Close behind is "saving resources for our children and grandchildren to use" in a dead heat with "providing a better life for our children and grandchildren."

46% think cutting fossil fuel use would improve people's health 43 % felt it would "protect God's Creation," and 41% said it would create jobs and strengthen our economy. 30 % said it would limit climate change or improve our national security.

The statistics from this poll indicate a somewhat surprising amount of conservatives who are on board with making changes regarding climate change. Notice, however that their motivations for change are planks right out the Republican playbook. This is a frustrating state of affairs.

It is shocking to learn that a majority of republicans and independents favor legislation and action to prevent climate change and yet there is such polarization among us.

This brings to mind my first political involvement on behalf of a California proposition on the ballot in 2012. The most watched environmental fight in the nation had conservation groups waging an all-out war against Valero Energy, the nation's largest independent oil refiner, Koch Industries and Tesoro Corp—all of whom back passage of the measure with millions of money from outside the state. As a member of VCCOOL (Ventura Climate Change Organization), I became actively involved in defeating this measure. I remember the first meeting at city hall with VCCOOL members and local officials to make plans. "Shock and Awe" is the best way to describe the reaction of the group when I revealed that I was the ONLY southern, conservative, evangelical, Republican in the room. At first, I'm sure they suspected that I was a spy. Very quickly they recognized me as a resource; a voice from the "dark side" who might be effective in helping to educate and inform those of my ilk. It was a fulfilling experience and a successful one.

CHAPTER 2

The heavens declare the glory of God; the skies proclaim the work of His hand."

— Psalm 19:1 —

ENVIRONMENTAL CONSIDERATIONS

GLOBAL WARMING

Global warming is the rise in the average temperature of Earth's atmosphere and oceans since the late 19th century and its projected continuation. Since the early 20th century, Earth's mean surface temperature has increased by about 1.4 °F with about two-thirds of the increase occurring since 1980. The Earth's atmosphere is overloaded with heat-trapping carbon dioxide, which threatens large-scale disruptions in climate with disastrous consequences. We must act now to spur the adoption of cleaner energy sources at home and abroad.

The causes, actions, and results of global warming are closely paralleled and even intertwined with Climate Change. A part of climate change is the warming of the earths surface and atmosphere.

At the outset we must remind ourselves that the "earth" is really over two-thirds ocean, as we learned early in grammar school. Today 60% of the earth's population lives within 60 miles of water. Throughout history, people have been living near and interacting with our oceans with the sense that nothing humans do could possibly effect this enormous watery world in any way. While humans were few in numbers, the oceans were able to withstand and absorb most of these destructive activities. The ocean is a very sensitive ecosystem and is now showing signs of imbalance from chronic overuse and abuse, thus contributing to global warming.

Carbon dioxide, nitrous oxide, and methane are the gases that cause global warming. Global warming is the steady increase in the average temperature of the Earth's atmosphere and its oceans. Its results are loss of lives and scarcity of food due to changing and harsh weather patterns. Global warming is caused by various factors. One factor is that the Earth's heat is trapped and therefore not dissipating as it should. Global Warming is caused by CFCs and air pollution. CFCs is the main cause. CFC stands for Chloro Fluoro Carbon which is widely used as solvent and refrigerant Burning fossil fuels. (coal, oil and natural gas) in industry transport and electricity generation. This adds carbon dioxide to the greenhouse gases.

Scientists have determined that a number of human activities. are contributing to global warming by adding excessive amounts of greenhouse gases to the atmosphere.

Some view that since global warming is a rise in average global temperature, it is part of natural heating and cooling global cycles which have existed for centuries.

Unfortunately, many divergent views are the core reason that it is difficult to get the opposing sides of the view together. Mixing facts with conjecture is not only confusing but also serves to create a deep distrust in ALL facts coming from credible environmental scientists. Varying views are essential to solving the problem. It is much like a world-wide laboratory where the elements and the facts collide and help us to draw conclusions— some correct, some false. It is important that those who interpret the facts examine all the data and not jump to conclusions. Even a child could ascertain that just because the first popsicle out of the box is grape that there is no guarantee that All the popsicle are grape. Some extremist views are the core reason that it is difficult to get any opposing views to be considered by administrators in the battle against global warming.

Major oil companies are also working internationally and at the U.S. federal and state levels to contribute to climate change policy discussions. They insist that their stance reflects a balanced approach to addressing climate change through short and long-term measures. As they work to reduce greenhouse gasses, our collective challenge is to create solutions that protect the environment without undermining the growth of the global economy. I believe that a successful climate policy will be one in which the reduction of greenhouse gasses is accomplished equitably by the top emitting countries of the world through long-term and coordinated national frameworks.

Many conservatives believe that the **global warming** theory is the liberal hoax that the world is becoming dangerously warmer due to the human pollution of greenhouse gasses, such as carbon dioxide, methane, and nitrous oxide. Liberals have used the theory of man-made global warming to seek rationing by government of life-saving energy production and consumption. Moreover, natural periods of global warming and global cooling are expected to occur regardless of human activity, and liberals are demanding more government control to combat an alleged cooling in temperatures, with some scientists warning of a possible ice age. Conservative "scientists" lay claim that the ease of refutation of global cooling claims foretells the eventual fate of the current global warming hysteria.

Political activists use the term "global warming" to refer to anthropogenic global warming theory (AGW), which asserts that human activity such as spewing "greenhouse gases" is causing an increase in temperature and is more significant than natural causes and cycles. The AGW theory is supported by left-leaning political parties, as well as a majority of sovereign states, national agencies, and an intergovernmental panel. The reality is that there seems to be no immediate global crisis, and even dire warnings by the UN's Intergovernmental Panel on Climate Change admit that significant effects will not be manifested for at least 100 years.

Today the scientific community is in almost total agreement that the earth's climate is changing and that this represents a huge threat to the planet and to us. According to a Pew survey , however, public opinion lags behind the scientific conclusion, with only 69% of those surveyed accepting the view that the earth is warming — and only 1 in 4 Americans see global warming as a major threat. Climate campaigners have long debated how to better communicate the message.

If it's not a data deficit that's preventing people from doing more on global warming, what is it? We face a minefield of mental barriers and issues that prevent us from confronting the threat. For some, the answer lies in cognitive science. Daniel Gilbert, a professor of psychology at Harvard, describes some key reasons; global warming doesn't take a human form, our brains' failure to accurately perceive gradual change as opposed to rapid shifts, climate change has occurred slowly enough for our minds to normalize it. Other reasons assume that ideologies or worldviews may prevent action, social comparisons with other people and perceived inequity (the "Why should we change if X corporation or Y country won't?") and the perceived risks of changing our behavior. Finally is the favorite cop out, "I'm only one person, what can I do?" For many, the first challenge will be in recognizing which dragons they have to deal with before they can overcome them. If you don't know what your problem is, you don't know what the solution is.

The key then, becomes one of motivation. The "smart, educated, and informed" scientific community observes with disdain and elitist pity upon the faith-based crowd of unschooled and ignorant who make a point of refusing to believe in "proven" science.

At this point I will interject my own personal beliefs: I am an evangelical Christian, creationist, conservative and believe that the Bible is the literal, Word of God. Yet, I in no way feel excused from my obligation to care for this wonderful world that we share. I do not need to debate any scientists about what I choose to believe regarding the infallibility of the Bible any more than a Buddhist, Hindu, Muslim, Jew should have to debate about their beliefs. And before the rebuff, those who may be atheistic, agnostic, pantheistic, or have no belief at all; while I wish you believed as I do, I respect your right to believe in something, or nothing.

The mainstream climate-change community has been slow to register the value of psychology in addressing global warming. Reading from Lertzman and Gifford and their attempts to analyze the "problem" in getting conservatives on board with Global Warming it strikes me as amusing that they actually use the terms "social analysis, shame, too big an abstract issue to deal with, pain, and psychological barriers" to come to grips with Conservative views.

I would recommend a quick trip through the Bible or other creationists literature so that such learned scientists could face an even more abstract idea: Faith. For readers who do not understand "faith" please work the simple mental exercise. If you are sitting, did you check the chair for its soundness before you sat down? Did you personally check your auto, bike, or public transit before you climbed on board? If you answered "no" then you exercised FAITH. You assumed the object would do what it was designed to do.

This scenario works both ways. Many conservative Christians can be hypocritical, sanctimonious, and so heavenly minded that they are not earthly good. A future chapter will deal exclusively with the problem of the "faithful" Bible believer who refuses to accept the mandate in God's Word to be stewards and caretakers of all of Creation. It is time to accept responsibility which more than likely will lead you to improve the environment and the quality of life on earth.

Getting both sides together should not be that difficult. Of course there are no doubt going to be some on both sides of the issue who will not budge, "on principle." On the religious right, with which I am familiar, legalistic, pharisaical dogma will prevent the most right-wing from even associating with those of differently perceived positions. (These were the same people who refused to integrate in the 1960's.)

On the left, you have the intelligent elite who really, just feel people who do not agree with them should go home. "slop the hogs" and not even try to get involved with a serious conservation.

CHAPTER 3

"Thank God men cannot fly, and lay waste the sky as well as the earth."

— *Henry David Thoreau —*

ENVIRONMENTAL CONSIDERATIONS

DEGRADING OZONE LAYER

The ozone layer is an atmospheric layer at heights of about 20 to 30 miles (32 to 48 kilometers) that is normally characterized by high ozone content which blocks most solar ultraviolet radiation from entry into the lower atmosphere. Certain industrial compounds, such as the refrigerant Freon for example, break down ozone in the stratosphere at very high rates for long periods of time. These compounds greatly reduce the ozone's ability to protect surface life from UV radiation. Ozone is a highly reactive molecule that contains three oxygen atoms. It is constantly being formed and broken down in the high atmosphere in the region called the stratosphere.

There is widespread concern that the ozone layer is deteriorating due to the release of pollution containing the chemicals chlorine and bromine. Such deterioration allows large amounts of ultraviolet B rays to reach Earth, which can cause skin cancer and cataracts in humans and harm animals as well.

Chlorofluorocarbons (CFCs), chemicals found mainly in spray aerosols heavily used by industrialized nations for much of the past 50 years, are the primary culprits in ozone layer breakdown. When CFCs reach the upper atmosphere, they are exposed to ultraviolet rays, which causes them to break down into substances that include chlorine. The chlorine reacts with the oxygen atoms in ozone and rips apart the ozone molecule. One atom of chlorine can destroy more than a hundred thousand ozone molecules, according to the U.S. Environmental Protection Agency. CFCs, which have a long history of use as refrigerants, solvents, foam-blowing agents and in other applications, have been almost completely phased out worldwide. In addition, restrictions are now in place to phase out hydro chlorofluorocarbons (HCFCs), compounds used as substitutes for the more damaging CFCs. The U.S. will phase out HCFCs completely in 2030.

What is EPA Doing About Ozone Layer Depletion?

♦ Ending production and use of ozone depleting substances.

♦ Ensuring that ozone depleting substances are recycled properly, and prohibiting unnecessary releases of these substances.

♦ Identifying safe alternatives through the Significant New Alternatives Policy (SNAP) program.

♦ Banning the release of ozone-depleting refrigerants during the service, maintenance, and disposal of air conditioners and other refrigeration equipment.

♦ Requiring that manufacturers label products containing or made with the most harmful ozone depleting substances.

Concerning the serious health threat posed by higher UV levels, the EPA is working with schools and communities across the nation through the SunWise Program. SunWise is an environmental and health education program that teaches children and their caregivers about ozone depletion, UV radiation, and how to protect themselves from overexposure to the sun.

Laboratory studies demonstrate that ultra violet short rays (UVB) cause non-melanoma skin cancer and plays a major role in malignant melanoma development. In addition, UVB has been linked to cataracts -- a clouding of the eye's lens. All sunlight contains some UVB, even with normal stratospheric ozone levels. It is always important to protect your skin and eyes from the sun. Ozone layer depletion increases the amount of UVB and the risk of health effects.

There is somewhat of a consensus of views of the importance of a consistent ozone layer above the earth and its importance to the earth and all life. Critics and skeptics, many industrial producers of CFCs and aerosol products, along with conservative think tanks have of course refuted the "theory" of these causes of ozone depletion.

Once again, years of global research by the scientific community was attacked immediately, led by the industries that would benefit the most from a discrediting of depleting ozone. A typical response would assert the following type explanation: "There is in fact an annual thinning then thickening of the ozone layer above the earth virtually every year. Efforts to decrease the ozone loss in the atmosphere would only decrease ozone loss by 5% in 50 years. In fact, different areas on the planet, a close as 100 miles apart have different thicknesses of ozone."

It is true that the ozone layer fluctuates from area to area and front season to season. Nevertheless, a huge hole in the layer located above the south pole appeared and grew to its largest size of over 10,000,000 square miles in September, 2006. The size has now decreased and is expected to disappear completely in the future. The argument again is if this accretion is due to compliance with strict CFC regulations or a purely natural occurrence.

Coming together should be simple. It seems unimaginable to think that anyone would insist on the continued use of items that are potentially harmful to the environment in order to prove a point. The industries around the world that felt they could not survive have adapted quite well, or thankfully, are now out of business.

FAILING BIODIVERSITY

Sustainable Me II

DYING OCEANS

ENDANGERED SPECIES

CHAPTER 4

"When one tugs at a single thing in nature,

He finds it attached to the rest of the world."

— John Muir —

FAILING BIODIVERSITY

DYING OCEANS

Our oceans are dying, decimated by over-fishing and devoid of over 95% of its larger predatory fish such as sharks and Bluefin Tuna. Tons upon tons of discarded plastic ends up in kill zones that cover hundreds of acres. This ocean trash kills and sickens marine life up and down the food chain. This garbage is slowly breaking down into micro pellets which will continue to cause harm for generations.

There is a need for a worldwide effort to regulate and enforce sustainable fishing practices. Acres of ocean plastic from shopping bags, to flip-flops, plastic bottles, industrial waste, toys, and dozens of other sources need to be cut off. Biodegradable plastics, not just those that break into smaller pieces need to be widely adopted.

A little over 25 years ago three people in Malibu, California found out that their favorite wave was about to be destroyed. Those three people organized and worked with the local municipalities until they were satisfied that their efforts to preserve that iconic wave would be successful. The Surfrider Association mission is the protection and enjoyment of oceans, waves and beaches through a powerful activist network that reaches around the world. They promote the right of low-impact, free and open access to the world's waves and beaches for all people.

Their Blue Water Task Force has demonstrated success by identifying problems with beach and coastal water pollution, and the Ocean Ecosystem Program protects and restores ocean ecosystems through a proactive approach. The Ocean Friendly Gardens Program educates and assists people in creating landscapes that utilize native plants, permeable groundcovers and water retention features to prevent urban runoff, create wildlife habitats and design beautiful spaces. This is what can happen when people see a problem and set about to correct it.

There are several other organizations that are worth mentioning. One is the California Ships to Reefs organization. Their vision is to establish a regional system of artificial reefs along the California coast to improve and enhance the California fish, plant and marine ecosystem, and to enhance the tourism industry centered on fishing and diving. "I think reefing ships is a fantastic win/win/win scenario for sport divers, sport fishermen and the environment.

Natural wrecks break down into rubble piles over time and though they will continue to attract fish, the bigger the structure the bigger the attraction and the bigger the ecosystem it will hold and or attract." - Richie Kohler, Advisory Board, Ships to Reefs International

Established in 1977, Sea Shepherd Conservation Society is an international non-profit, marine wildlife conservation organization. They seek to end the destruction of habitat and slaughter of wildlife in the world's oceans. Sea Shepherd uses innovative direct-action tactics to investigate, document, and take action to expose and confront illegal activities in the oceans. By safeguarding the biodiversity of our delicately balanced ocean ecosystems, Sea Shepherd works to ensure their survival for future generations. The oceans are under siege by a "deadly trio" of threats — rising water temperature, acidification, and lack of oxygen This time, humans are largely to blame, and apart from the moral failures involved, our negligence will have profound effects on humanity's future.

Overfishing alone has pushed many species to the brink of extinction. Pollution and run-off of fertilizers from farms have choked out life in vast areas. And the oceans absorb most of the carbon dioxide we pump into the atmosphere, changing PH levels and adding stress on all kinds of marine creatures. However, unlike climate change, these problems can be directly, immediately and effectively tackled by policy change. Tracking of results will produce data that is accurate and verifiable.

Life in the ocean comprises more major taxonomic groups (phyla), which represent separate evolutionary paths, than does life on land. It is therefore certain that in the ocean there are more species that are very different from each other, although it is not yet known which realm has the most species.

Because so much of the ocean is only accessible with expensive technology and/or remote instrumentation, uncovering the extent of marine biodiversity has been and continues to be a slow and difficult undertaking. Much of ocean life remains a mystery and there are an unknown number of species yet to be discovered.

It is also difficult to determine the status of most species in the ocean. So little is known of many species' distribution or range that it cannot be determined whether they are plentiful or naturally rare or whether populations are stable or changing, and if they are threatened or endangered. Because there is little evidence to the contrary, there has been a common impression that marine species and ecosystems are generally in good shape. However, as more is learned, that impression is turning out to be wildly misconceived.

Our lack of knowledge about oceanic species eliminates much of the grounds for debate over dealing with potential problems. One thing for sure is that if we can see loss of biodiversity among sea life throughout known species; then we may expect that the same toxins are negatively affecting those yet to be discovered.

CHAPTER 5

"Uniformity is not nature's way; Diversity is nature's way."

— Vandana Shiva —

FAILING BIODIVERSITY

ENDANGERED SPECIES

Within the last century our activities as humans is responsible for rapidly diminishing life forms on earth. Conservative estimates are that dozens of species are going extinct each day. This alarming fact is accelerating as natural habitats shrink, fragment, and degrade and commercial exploitation of vulnerable species increases. The loss of species and destruction of their natural habitats is irreversible.

The escalating sciences of Biomimicry, bioengineering and genetic manipulations underscore the huge potential a single species can make in helping to build a more sustainable environment.

So far our efforts have been feeble. A good start would be to fully shut down the international trade in wildlife, protect remaining habitats, and begin to restore watersheds by removing dams and protecting headwater and riverbank vegetation.

According to the World Wildlife Fund, a leading organization established in 1961 as an international fundraising organization to work in collaboration with existing conservation groups and bring substantial financial support to the conservation movement on a worldwide scale. There is an extensive list of nearly 100 endangered species on their web site. Some are listed as "least concern," "near threatened," "vulnerable," or "endangered." The group that is of most concern are those species that are considered literally on the brink of extinction and thus are in a "critical" state of endangerment. The chart on the next page is a part of the list from the National Wildlife Fund, who works with other organizations and governments around the world to prevent extinction of endangered species.

CRITICALLY ENDANGERED SPECIES

Common name	Scientific name
Amur Leopard	Panthera pardus orientalis
Black Rhino	Diceros bicornis
Cross River Gorilla	Gorilla gorilla diehli
Hawksbill Turtle	Eretmochelys imbricata
Javan Rhino	Rhinoceros sondaicus
Leatherback Turtle	Dermochelys coriacea
Mountain Gorilla	Gorilla beringei beringei
Saola	Pseudoryx nghetinhensis
South China Tiger	Panthera tigris amoyensis
Sumatran Elephant	Elephas maximus sumatranus
Sumatran Orangutan	Pongo abelii
Sumatran Rhino	Dicerorhinus sumatrensis
Sumatran Tiger	Panthera tigris sumatrae
Vaquita	Phocoena sinus
Western Lowland Gorilla	Gorilla gorilla
Yangtze Finless Porpoise	Neophocaena asiaeorientalis ssp.

The United States Fish and Wildlife Service , paid for by tax dollars has cataloged a large group of plants and animals that are considered either endangered or threatened. Their list includes the following :

ENDANGERED SPECIES IN THE U.S.

Group	Endangered	Threatened	Total Listings	Listings with Recovery
Mammals	69	16	85	62
Birds	78	15	93	86
Reptiles	14	22	36	35
Amphibians	17	11	28	17
Fishes	84	70	154	102
Clams	72	12	84	71
Snails	33	13	46	30
Millipedes	0	0	0	0
Insects	57	10	67	40
Arachnids	12	0	12	12
Crustaceans	20	3	23	18
Animal	456	172	628	473
Flowering	669	150	819	641
Conifers and Cycads	2	1	3	3
Ferns and	28	2	30	26
Lichens	2	0	2	2
Plant totals	701	153	854	672
Grand totals	1157	327	1484	1145

The conservation status of a species is an indicator of the likelihood of that endangered species becoming extinct. Many factors are taken into account when assessing statistics such as the number remaining, the overall increase or decrease in the population over time, breeding success rates, known threats, and so on. The International Union for Conservation of Nature's Red List of Threatened Species is the best-known worldwide conservation status listing and ranking system. It has been estimated that over 40% of all living species on Earth are at risk of going extinct. Internationally, 199 countries have signed an accord agreeing to create Biodiversity Action Plans to protect endangered and other threatened species. In the United States this plan is usually called a species Recovery Plan.

Politically, most conservatives and liberals seem to agree that we should protect the wealth of plants and animals. However, there are still areas of major conflict and confusion when it comes to species threats. Some endangered species laws are controversial. Typical areas of controversy include: criteria for placing a species on the endangered species list, and criteria for removing a species from the list once its population has recovered; whether restrictions on land development constitute a "taking" of land by the government; the related question of whether private landowners should be compensated for the loss of uses of their lands; and obtaining reasonable exceptions to protection laws. Also lobbying from hunters and various industries like the petroleum industry, construction industry, and logging, has been an obstacle in establishing endangered species laws.

In one of the fastest growing cities in America, Bakersfield, California, challenges have been reckoned with as the number of new housing developments, schools and shopping centers grows exponentially. Having lived there for over 25 years I have seen the number of high schools grow from 7 in the late '80s to over 20 to date. All this growth was predicated on the whereabouts of 15 endangered species, 13 threatened species and 69 species of concern. The hot and dry basin of the southern San Joaquin Valley often watched projects come to a standstill until a slender salamander was studied or a pair of rare kit foxes raised their young. Typically the media paid little attention to the plight of the endangered species but showed a great deal of concern for the halting of economic "progress." This is a scenario that is played over every day in cities and towns across America and around the world.

The conflict is a difficult one to resolve because of the demands by consumers and population expansion. In areas with an abundance of agriculture, business growth, fossil fuel production, or major industry you would be had pressed to find a political leader from either major party on any level of government with the boldness to stand up for any endangered species in the face of such opposition.

The number of species of plants, animals, and microorganisms, the enormous diversity of genes in these species, the different ecosystems on the planet, such as deserts, rainforests and coral reefs are all part of a biologically diverse Earth. Appropriate conservation and sustainable development strategies attempt to recognize this as being integral to any approach.

We must understand the inventory of biodiversity and the interactions between different species, make a thorough diagnosis of the dangers that threaten biodiversity, and find solutions to protect it and restore what human activity has destroyed. Some challenges for the future of our planet's biodiversity are:

♦ Understanding and communicating the value of Biodiversity

♦ Protecting our natural heritage, physical and biological

♦ Setting limits for human incursion in the Biosphere

♦ Preserving Sustainable resources

♦ Recreating Biomes of diversity where needed

In part, our failing biodiversity is due to the capacity of eco-systems to produce useful biological materials and to absorb waste materials that are generated by humans. This is know as biocapacity. While is sounds similar, it is not the same as an ecological footprint. A biocapacity deficit occurs when a nation (city or any other region) has a carbon footprint that exceeds the biocapacity available to the population of that area.

The ecological footprint is a measure of human demand on the Earth. It is a standardized measure of demand for natural resources that may be contrasted with the planet's capacity to regenerate. It has to do with the amount of biologically productive land and sea area needed to supply the resources the population consumes.

One of the most successful ways to contribute to a healthier and more bio-diverse earth is to partner with non-profits and government organizations. There are hundreds of non-profits on the global, national, state and local levels that may speak to you in a personal way. If so, get involved by donations, volunteering, or spreading the work.

Everything that lives in an ecosystem is part of the web of life. Each species of vegetation and each creature has a place on the earth and plays a vital role in the circle of life. Maintaining a wide diversity of species in each ecosystem is necessary to preserve the web of life that sustains all living things

ENERGY

Sustainable Me II

NUCLEAR ENERGY

FOSSIL FUELS

Ben Thomas

CHAPTER 6

"A mind stretched by a new idea

can never go back to its original dimension"

— *Oliver Wendell Holmes* —

ENERGY

NUCLEAR ENERGY

Nuclear power is the use of sustained nuclear fission to generate heat and electricity. Nuclear power accounts for about 6% of the world's energy and 13% of the world's electricity. The United States, France, and Japan together account for about 50% of nuclear generated electricity. There are over 400 nuclear power reactors in operation around the world in over 30 countries. We will not take into account for this discussion nuclear powered ships or weapons of mass destruction located all over our planet.

Nuclear energy relies on the fact that some elements can be split (the process of fission) and will release part of their energy as heat. Uranium-235 fissions easily and is most commonly used with Uranium-238. The power plant generate electricity like other steam-electric power plants. Heated water becomes steam which turns turbines and generates electricity. In other plants coal, oil or gas is burned to produce the steam and produce the power.

Plutonium is a waste product of nuclear fission which can power plants or be used in bombs. Less than 8 kilograms (18 pounds) of plutonium is enough for one Nagasaki-type bomb.

Mining uranium, it's refining and enrichment and producing plutonium yield radioactive isotopes that contaminate the surrounding environment. The entire ecosystem are adversely affected. Some of these radioactive isotopes are extraordinarily long-lived, remaining toxic for hundreds of thousands of years. Presently, we are only beginning to observe and experience the consequences of producing nuclear energy.

Nuclear power has at least four waste streams that may harm the environment:

♦ Spent nuclear fuel at the reactor site (including fission products and plutonium waste)

♦ Tailings and waste rock at uranium mines and mills

♦ Releases of small amounts of radioactive isotopes during reactor operation

♦ Releases of large quantities of dangerous radioactive materials during accidents

Although opponents cry "foul" there are many intelligent scientists and advocates of nuclear energy as the "clean and safe" choice for a world choking on other environmentally "dirty" methods of producing electricity. Nuclear energy already provides 70 percent of the country's emission-free electricity. With America's electricity needs forecast to grow 22 % by 2035, America's future energy demands will require a broad portfolio of energy solutions, and nuclear must be a part of the energy mix. CASEnergy activates voices of support among the coalition's co-chairs and 2,800+ members who represent a diverse group of individuals and organizations from the business, academic, industry, consumer, minority and labor communities.

Clean and Safe Energy Coalition is a national grassroots organization that supports the increased use of nuclear energy to ensure an affordable, environmentally clean, reliable and safe supply of electricity. Funded by the industry, the coalition was formed in 2006 to inform the public dialogue and educate Americans on the many benefits of nuclear energy.

Arguments for the use of nuclear power:

♦ Nuclear power is clean: Over its life-cycle, a nuclear power station will emit around 50 tons of CO_2 per gigawatt hour of electricity generated, compared with nearly 500 tons from gas and over 900 tons from coal.

57

♦ Nuclear power is cheap: When the Government's carbon price and the cost of intermittent supply from renewables are taken into account, we could expect electricity from a nuclear plant built in the near future to cost much less. Gas power would cost 35% more, coal 85% more and wind from 105% (on-shore) to 135% (off-shore).

♦ Nuclear power is safe: The European Commission has identified nuclear as the safest form of electricity generation, causing relatively fewer deaths (0-0.2 deaths per gigawatt year of electricity generated) than wind (0.2 deaths), hydroelectric (0-0.8), gas (0.1-0.4), peat and biomass (1.4), coal (2.8) and oil (4.1).

It is quite obvious that this issue is highly polarized and one that is the source of contentious debate. It is also an issue that does not seem to divide along political or religious lines. I will admit that when I drive past a nuclear power plant that I do not have the same reaction as when I pass an electric plant powered by fossil fuels. I think it is the vision of a giant chimney belching forth billows of dirty smoke that is the big turn-off. On the other hand, I never plan to live anywhere near a nuclear power plant—or any other power plant. Perhaps I am inconsistent but I can say that I'm honest on this issue.

There are few areas of agreement from the nuclear and NO-nuclear positions. Perhaps we could say that neither side likes coal or fossil fuels. Most environmentalists would prefer natural power sources such as solar or wind power—both clean and safe. Low-carbon power comes from processes or technologies that produce power with substantially lower amounts of carbon dioxide emissions than is presently emitted from conventional fossil fuel power generation. It includes low carbon power generation sources such as wind power, solar power and Hydro power. Although Hydro power is clean, it is not in favor with the eco-conscious because it involves building dams and inundating entire eco-systems and displacing thousands of animals.

CHAPTER 7

"Vision without action is a daydream.

Action without vision is a nightmare."

— *Japanese Proverb* —

ENERGY

FOSSIL FUELS

Fossil fuels are hydrocarbons, primarily coal, fuel oil or natural gas, formed from the remains of dead plants and animals. Fossil fuel is a term for buried combustible geologic deposits of organic materials. The burning of fossil fuels by humans is the largest source of emissions of carbon dioxide, which is one of the greenhouse gases that contributes to global warming. They range from volatile materials with low carbon/hydrogen ratios like methane, to liquid petroleum to nonvolatile materials composed of almost pure carbon, like anthracite coal.

A small portion of hydrocarbon-based fuels are biofuels derived from atmospheric carbon dioxide, and thus do not increase the net amount of carbon dioxide in the atmosphere.

Fossil fuels are of great importance because they can be burned, producing significant amounts of energy per unit weight. The use of coal as a fuel predates recorded history. Coal was used in ancient times to run furnaces for the melting of metal ore. The U.S. holds less than 5% of the world's population, but due to large houses and private cars, uses more than a quarter of the world's supply of fossil fuels. In the United States, more than 90% of greenhouse gas emissions come from the combustion of fossil fuels which also produces other air pollutants, such as nitrogen oxides, sulfur dioxide, volatile organic compounds and heavy metals. Burning coal also generates large amounts of ash that is used in a wide variety of applications, utilizing about 40% of the US production

As a result of their origins, fossil fuels have a very high carbon content, which is the building block element of living things. This is one source of danger from fossil fuels.

Just as you might expect, combustion or burning of fossil fuels results in the release of many chemicals in the form of smoke, soot, or more technically, fly ash. According to the Environmental Protection Agency, or EPA, coal powers 52 percent of electric power plants in the U.S. because it is plentiful and relatively cheap.

However, it also contains many impurities, some of which escape into the air, causing particulate pollution that can lodge deep in the lungs.

All types of fossil fuels emit carbon dioxide, CO_2, when they are burned, and according to the EPA, fossil fuels are the largest source of CO_2 globally. Carbon dioxide is the most significant greenhouse gas, which contributes to warming the Earth's atmosphere.

Petroleum is the fossil fuel that is used virtually exclusively to produce transportation fuels: gasoline, diesel and jet fuel. Some industry analysts believe that worldwide oil production is declining, which is forcing oil companies to seek new deposits in more difficult environments, such as offshore or in fragile environmental areas.

Fossil fuels like coal and natural gas are natural resources. The U.S. Environmental Protection Agency warns that they're not renewable and can't be replenished, unlike renewable energy sources like solar or wind energy.

The particles released by burning fossil fuels contribute to air pollution, which leads to numerous potential health problems. The U.S. National Institute of Environmental Health Sciences says this includes low lung functioning, chronic asthma, cardiovascular disease and chronic bronchitis.

More than half of the petroleum that the United States uses is imported from foreign sources, according to the U.S Department of Energy. Depending on other countries for your fossil fuel energy, including many Middle Eastern countries, presents a security issue for the U.S. Countries can use their hold on America's fossil fuel supplies as a potent political bargaining chip, potentially putting the U.S.'s national concerns at risk.

We can not enter a discussion about fossil fuels without a mention of the latest trend in obtaining fuel. Hydraulic fracturing, or *"fracking"*, is the process of drilling and injecting fluid into the ground at a high pressure in order to fracture shale rocks to release natural gas inside.   As of 2010, it was estimated that 60% of all new oil and gas wells worldwide were being hydraulically fractured.

Proponents of hydraulic fracturing point to the economic benefits from the vast amounts of formerly inaccessible hydrocarbons the process can extract. Opponents point to potential environmental impacts, including contamination of ground water, depletion of fresh water, risks to air quality, noise pollution, the migration of gases and hydraulic fracturing chemicals to the surface, surface contamination from spills and flow-back, and the health effects of these.

Several organizations, researchers, and media outlets have reported difficulty in conducting and reporting the results of studies on hydraulic fracturing due to industry and governmental pressure, and expressed concern over possible censoring of environmental reports. The broader debate over these topics provides an example of the research challenges on this subject.

Wastewater from the controversial practice of fracking appears to be linked to all the earthquakes in a town in Ohio that had no known past quakes, research now reveals. The practice of hydraulic fracturing, or fracking opens up fissures that help oil and natural gas flow out more freely. This process generates wastewater that is often pumped underground as well, in order to get rid of it and the movement of earth it appears, may be the cause of earthquakes as well. A furious debate has erupted over the safety of the practice.

Advocates claim fracking is a safe, economical source of clean energy, while critics argue that it can taint drinking water supplies, among other problems. Fracking is inherently unsafe and we cannot rely on regulation to protect communities' water, air and public health. The industry enjoys exemptions from key federal legislation protecting our air and water, thanks to aggressive lobbying.

Of course there are many who believe that the use of fossil fuels is the correct answer to the energy supply question. A major advantage of fossil fuels is their capacity to generate huge amounts of electricity in just a single location and they are very easy to find.

When coal is used in power plants, they are very cost effective. Transporting oil and gas to the power stations can be made through the use of pipes making it an easy task. Power plants that utilize gas are very efficient. Power stations that make use of fossil fuel can be constructed in almost any location.

Fossil fuels are easily combustible. Most combustion engines need to be powered with a little amount of fuel and they can produce a large amount of energy. Fossil fuels have been serving us for centuries. It is considered as a portable form of energy.

The fossil fuels are composed of the molecules of carbon, and hydrogen. This makes them very stable. Fossil fuels, due to their constancy and the constitution of the molecules are easy to store as well. They do not form any other compound if stored in the cans for a long time. For the same reason, transporting fossil fuels is also less difficult than any other form of fuels.

We now have the advantage of hybrid vehicles as well as gas motors with eco-boost features. Even with higher prices at the pump and a hypocritical disdain for petroleum powered vehicles, Americans can't resist the opportunity to drive—everywhere.

The battle, more often than not, pairs Republicans with big oil corporations against Democrats, the liberal left, and environmentalists. The problem facing the anti-fossil fuel advocates is that they very often do not practice what they preach. I am glad to notice that eco-conscious individuals are more consistent in using alternative forms of transportation (walk, bike, mass transit, for example). When it comes to the politicians, the liberal elite, and the entertainment world; there is a lot more advocacy and a lot less follow through. I am disappointed each time I see a Hollywood personality or music mogul pull up to an environmental event which likely wastes tons of food in a limo that brought them from their private jet or their massive non-energy friendly home. There is no excuse.

The solution to our fossil fuel dependence and it's ties to the middle east is to consider alternative fuels and energy sources for our vehicles and homes. There are a few areas on which we can agree as a starting point. First, economics: driving less means using less fuel. Simple Economics 101 teaches about "supply and demand." If we reduce demand we will reduce dependence on foreign oil and hopefully lower prices at the pump. Second, walking or riding a bike is a much healthier way to commute to *wherever* we need to go. Next, the use of alternative energy at home can save hundreds of dollars per year. Making your home energy efficient will also reduce your need for fossil fuels it that is what powers your heat.

Let's shift the conversation to a variety of energy options. There are many alternative energy sources that are sustainable and do not pose the accident risks inherent in nuclear energy production nor the pollution problems of fossil fuels . These sources include:

- Bioenergy: biomass, such as plant matter and animal waste, can yield power, heat, steam, and fuel.
- Geothermal: renewable heat energy can be harnessed from deep within the earth.
- Wind: turbines turning in the air convert kinetic energy in the wind into electricity.
- Solar: the sun's energy can be captured and used to produce heat and electricity.
- Hydrogen: if produced by renewable sources, it can power fuel cells to convert chemical energy directly into electricity, with useful heat and water as the only byproducts.
- Tidal: using the movement of the ocean to power turbines and generate electricity.

Many more sustainable resources could be found and current resources improved if better technology were available and if the government and utilities actively promoted their development.

Emissions trading or "cap and trade" is a market-based approach used to control pollution by providing economic incentives for achieving reductions in the emissions of pollutants. People now call that system "cap-and-trade." In the 1980s it was referred to as "emissions trading," though some people called it "morally bankrupt" or even "a license to kill." For a strange alliance of free-market Republicans and renegade environmentalists, it represented a very novel approach to cleaning up the world—by working with human nature instead of against it.

Getting all this to work in the real world required a leap of faith. The opportunity came with the 1988 election of George H.W. Bush. Environmental Defense Fund (EDF) president Fred Krupp phoned the Bush White House and suggested that the best way for Bush to make good on his pledge to become the "environmental president" was to fix the acid rain problem, and the best way to do that was by using the new tool of emissions trading. Gray liked the marketplace approach But global warming had now also registered as front-page news.   EDF and the Bush White House both felt from the start that emissions trading would ultimately be the best way to address this much larger challenge.

Coming together on most issues will take some diplomacy and a commitment of working together from both sides of the aisle.. Making the right choices is not always as easy as flipping a switch— and then there are the issue of personal pride, daring to cross political party lines or simply embarrassment at changing positions. Cap and Trade is a good example of coming together—awkwardly— but it accomplishes the dual tasks of polluting emission control and ac-countability. Perhaps there are yet more areas of commonality for us to explore on our path towards greener energy.

Ben Thomas

TOXINS

Sustainable Me II

GENETICALLY MODIFIED ORGANISMS

INSECTICIDES AND PESTICIDES

CHAPTER 8

"Treat the Earth well. It was not given to you by your parents. It was loaned to you by your children."

— Kenyan Proverb —

TOXINS

GMOS

GMOs, or "genetically modified organisms," are plants or animals that have been genetically engineered with DNA from bacteria, viruses or other plants and animals. Any GMO is an organism whose genetic material has been altered. Organisms that have been genetically modified include micro-organisms such as bacteria and yeast, insects, plants, fish, and mammals. GMOs are the source of genetically modified foods, and are also widely used in scientific research and to produce goods other than food. These experimental combinations of genes from different species cannot occur in nature or in traditional crossbreeding.

When genes are inserted, they usually come from a different species, which is a form of horizontal gene transfer. In nature this can occur when exogenous DNA penetrates the cell membrane for any reason. GMOs are used in biological and medical research, production of pharmaceutical drugs, experimental medicine , and agriculture. Virtually all commercial GMOs are engineered to withstand direct application of herbicide and/or to produce an insecticide. Despite biotech industry promises, none of the GMO traits currently on the market offer increased yield, drought tolerance, enhanced nutrition, or any other consumer benefit.

So, why all the concern about GMOs in foods and other products?   A growing body of evidence connects GMOs with health problems, environmental damage and violation of farmers' and consumers' rights. Most developed nations do not consider GMOs to be safe. In more than 60 countries around the world there are significant restrictions or outright bans on the production and sale of GMOs. In the U.S., the government has approved GMOs based on studies conducted by the same corporations that created them and profit from their sale.

In the U.S., GMOs are in as much as 80% of conventional processed food. The four major genetically modified crops are corn, cotton, soy beans, and canola. Several animal studies indicate serious health risks associated with GM food, including infertility, immune problems, accelerated aging, faulty insulin regulation, and changes in major organs and the gastrointestinal system. Before the FDA decided to allow GMOs into food without labeling, FDA scientists had repeatedly warned that GM foods can create unpredictable, hard-to-detect side effects, including allergies, toxins, new diseases, and problems.

More and more studies point to the idea that there's grave cause for concern about the health effects of consuming GMOs and the chemicals they are sprayed with, including food allergies, irritable bowels, organ damage, and cancer. Genetically modified crops include alfalfa, canola, corn, cotton, papaya, soy, sugar beets, zucchini and yellow summer squash. Also high-risk animal products are of concern (i.e. milk, meat, eggs, honey, etc.) because of contamination in feed. Since no GMO labeling is required in the United States, your best bet is to look for the USDA Certified Organic label.

Genetic modification of crops should be viewed in the light of what has gone on before. Mankind has been manipulating the genetics of crops for around 10,000 years. For example, wheat, the world's major crop is a hybrid of many different species. Genetically modified technology is the only technology to be regulated from its inception, before any mishaps had occurred..

Arguments in favor of the use and development of Genetically Engineered foods are being touted by huge corporations and farming interests such as DuPont and Monsanto. Following is a list of reasons that are being used to support GMO research and use in farming:

♦ GMOs Will Help End World Hunger

♦ GMOs Will Make Food Better—Pest and Disease Resistant

♦ GMOs are Safe

♦ GMOs Promote Agricultural Diversity

♦ GMOs are Backed by the FDA

In this debate there is little room for agreement. There are three groups in the forum: Those who support GMOs, those who simply don't care and those who are alarmed by the incursion of genetically engineered food products. Supporters like the term genetically "modified" as opposed to "engineered" because it sounds more earth-friendly and less laboratory engineered, which it is. They also see it as a huge money-making opportunity for themselves. They will be able to produce more drought tolerant, larger, healthier, and insect and pest resistant crops on corporate farms and around the world in developing third-world countries.

Opponents see things such as inserting genetic material from fish into tomatoes as an example of many "unnatural" procedures that when ingested by humans could have drastic effects. In nations such as Japan and the European Union GMOs must be labeled because all preliminary lab work shows harmful effects on the animals tested. The concern also goes to animal feeds that contain GMOs as this produces meat, milk, butter, cheese, and other animal byproducts with transferred GMOs.

The real outcome of this huge debate may take years to be told—as a generation of GMO consumers grow to maturity and old age. A question that must be answered is whether any of us would willingly volunteer to be part of a lab test such as this. Yet, this begs another question — Why would the government turn it's head and refuse to mandate labeling of food products that contain GMOs? I for one would like to know the contents of my food.

At one time we only worried about preservatives in canned, packaged and frozen foods. Now, even "fresh" fruit and vegetables are also at risk of containing GMOs whose use is suspect if not truly harmful to humans. The safest bet is to grow your own with non-GMO seed or plants or to buy USDA Certified Organic.

Ben Thomas

CHAPTER 9

"Study nature, love nature,
stay close to nature. It will never fail you."

— Frank Lloyd Wright —

TOXINS

INSECTICIDES and PESTICIDES

An insecticide is a chemical used against insects. They include components used against the eggs and larvae of insects respectively. Insecticides are used in agriculture, medicine, industry, and general home use. Insecticides are incorporated by treated plants. Insects ingest the insecticide while feeding on the plants or are destroyed upon contact.

Some insecticides kill or harm other creatures in addition to those they are intended to kill. For example, birds may be poisoned when they eat food that was recently sprayed with insecticides or when they mistake insecticide granules on the ground for food and eat it. Sprayed insecticides may drift from the area to which it is applied and into wildlife areas, especially when it is sprayed aerially.

Pesticides are substances meant for preventing or destroying any pest. Their most common use is as plant protection products. These products protect plants from damaging influences such as weeds, diseases or insects. Target pests can include insects, weeds, mollusks, birds, mammals, fish, roundworms and microbes that destroy property and spread disease.

Crop protection technology helps control the thousands of weed species, harmful insects and numerous plant diseases that afflict crops. Without these important crop protection and pest control technologies, U.S. food production would decline, many fruits and vegetables would be in short supply. This would in turn cause an increase and the price of food would rise. What's more, America's production of important fibers for clothing, such as cotton, would decrease as farmers would lose their harvests and livelihoods to crop pests and diseases.

Many pesticides cause similar reactions to those produced by insecticides. Pesticide poisoning occurs when chemicals intended to control a pest affect non-target organisms such as humans, wildlife, or bees. Mild Poisoning or Early Symptoms of Acute Poisoning may include the following: headache, fatigue, weakness, dizziness, restlessness, nervousness, perspiration, nausea, diarrhea, loss of appetite, loss of weight, thirst, moodiness, soreness in joints, skin irritation, eye irritation or irritation of the nose and throat.

The term pesticide also includes these substances:

♦ Defoliants : Cause leaves or other foliage to drop from a plant

♦ Desiccants : Promote drying of living tissues, such as plant tops.

♦ Insect growth regulators : Disrupt the molting or other life processes of insects.

♦ Plant growth regulators : Substances that alter expected growth, flowering, or reproduction rate of plants.

Exposure to insecticides can occur by ingestion, inhalation, or exposure to skin or eyes. The chemicals are absorbed through the skin, lungs, and gastrointestinal tract, then distributed among body tissues. The body may manifest many symptoms: vomiting, nausea, bowel irregularity, coughing, wheezing, difficulty breathing, blurred vision, tearing, slowed heart rate, lowered blood pressure, urinary and central nervous problems, to name a few.

Ever since pesticides have been available, society has been concerned about the risks associated with their use. While it is true that there are often environmental and health risks with using pesticides, there are also risks involved in many activities in our daily lives, such as driving an automobile or riding a bicycle on a busy street. On the other hand, there may be grave risks associated with letting certain pests go uncontrolled.

Positive uses of pesticides include several critical issues that affect humans:

- Mosquitoes vector diseases, like West Nile Virus, to humans.
- Termites cause serious damage to our structures and are costly to eliminate.
- Fire ants cause painful stings and may kill livestock.
- Vegetable producers may have blemished produce rejected because of not applying a fungicide to protect their crop.
- Without herbicides, vegetation that is left uncontrolled along our rights-of-way   can cause damage to our roads, limit the line of sight of drivers, and cause power outages in utility line corridors.
- Some potential pests, such as the Mediterranean fruit fly, would devastate the agricultural industry

Most people would acknowledge that the benefits of pesticides in today's society outweigh the risks associated with their use, especially when the risks are identified and kept under control. By controlling certain factors associated with risk, we more readily accept a practice.

Pesticides and insecticides are carefully controlled by the government. All EPA-approved pesticides must bear a label telling the consumer how to use the product correctly, legally and safely. A label is an extremely important document, one that should be read carefully by every end user.

We can not leave this discussion without the mention of one of the most pivotal insecticides ever developed in history, DDT (dichlorodiphenyltrichloroethane). First synthesized in 1874, DDT's insecticidal properties were not discovered until 1939, and it was used with great success in the second half of World War II to control malaria and typhus among civilians and troops.

In 1962, Silent Spring by American biologist Rachel Carson was published, cataloging the environmental impacts of the indiscriminate spraying of DDT and questioned the logic of releasing large amounts of chemicals into the environment without fully understanding their effects on ecology or human health. The book suggested that DDT and other pesticides may cause cancer and that their agricultural use was a threat to wildlife, particularly birds. Its publication was a signature event in the birth of the environmental movement. It resulted in a large public outcry that eventually led to DDT being banned for agricultural use in the US in 1972.

After consideration of both the benefits and dangers of using insecticides and pesticides the environmentally conscious is left to come to a logical conclusion: situational ethics must carefully prevail. On a smaller scale of the back yard or community garden, running the risk of pesticide use does not seem worth the risk.

Families garden and children play — there is no need to expose anyone to toxic poisons unnecessarily. In my first volume, "Sustainable Me: Green Tips and Terms for the Environmentally Conscious," in the Landscape and Garden chapter I discuss many "natural" options to weed and pest control. One method is planting flowers in the garden that attract insects or birds that feed on pests. This is beautiful, practical, and effective.

Mosquitos and other disease carrying pests often need to be chemically eradicated in the most sustainable means possible. Recent epidemics of the West Nile Virus, for example, which were causing dozens of deaths and threatening the population, had to be eradicated by the most effective means possible — and quickly. Yet we must be careful as these toxins are distributed.

Pesticides that are sprayed onto crops via tractors or airplanes must always consider the factor of the wind and the proximity of any farm workers in the area. My eldest son works with the Department of Agriculture in California's San Joaquin Valley. Many times during the planting and growth season of crops he is called out to work with the EPA to access what chemicals were sprayed, where they came from, and what treatments are recommended for people affected by them.

The takeaway here is that we should all work together in order to discover less toxic means of dealing with the effects of plant protection products. Not only the plants, but the entire environment as well as the human population must be protected.

In the U.S., the Environmental Protection Agency (EPA) has primary authority to register and regulate pesticides, authorized by several federal laws including the:

♦ Federal Insecticide, Fungicide, and Rodenticide Act (FIFRA) — allows EPA to register pesticides using risk/benefit standards (how much risk is balanced by how much benefit?);

♦ Federal Food, Drug, and Cosmetic Act (FFDCA) — aims to increase protection for children and infants, setting tolerances (maximum residues on food);

♦ Food Quality Protection Act of 1996 (FQPA) — amends the previous laws by establishing a single safety standard for tolerances — not risk/benefit — to increase protection of children from aggregate exposures (dietary, water and residential); adds a 10-fold safety factor and requires ongoing review of registrations; and the Endangered Species Act of 1973 — requires that pesticides that will harm these species will not be registered.

Ben Thomas

86

INROADS TO THE RIGHT

Sustainable Me II

THE PLAYERS

A BIBLICAL MANDATE FOR ENVIRONMENTALISM

CHAPTER 10

"Throughout the country that you hold

as a possession, you must provide for

the redemption of the land."

— Leviticus 25:24 —

INROADS TO THE RIGHT

THE PLAYERS

There are various inroads currently being made into what we could refer to as the right wing conservative movement. I am such a person. Here is the short list of Republicans who are taking a stand for environmentalism:

*1. _____

To me, an ENVIRONMENTAL, evangelical, conservative Republican, this is quite shocking and a total embarrassment. I can only hope that there are more who share my concerns that will take a stand for environmental causes.

Fortunately churches are getting more in tune with the environmental movement. After 1,500 years the Vatican has brought the seven deadly sins up to date by adding seven new ones for the age of globalization. The new deadly sins include *polluting*, *genetic engineering*, being obscenely rich, drug dealing, abortion, pedophilia and <u>causing social injustice</u>. Notice that three of the seven are directly related to eco-consciousness.

Leaders from Christian, Jewish, Muslim, Hindu, Sikh, Buddhist, Baha'i, Jain and Zoroastrian faiths called on the UK and G20 governments to fight for an ambitious deal to cut greenhouse gas emissions saying that the survival of the poor and needy people of earth and our fragile creation depend on aggressive action.

A prevalent view among evangelicals that explain the overall lack of ardor for environmentalism is dominionism and the view of limited role of government and that God gave humans dominion over the earth. It would be assumed that this evangelical conservative group would follow through with more outward expressions of concern for the "Creation" and actions that show their obedience to the Biblical mandate of dominion over the earth. Creationist or Evolutionist? The earth remains the same. We inhabit it and are responsible for its care.

Southern Baptist leaders have just recently changed their tune on global warming. After years of casting serious doubt on humans being responsible for global warming, several prominent leaders in the Southern Baptist Convention (the largest Protestant denomination in the United States) have stated that Baptists have a moral responsibility to fight climate change. Their former lack of response to these issues in the face of mounting evidence may be seen by the world as uncaring, reckless and ill-informed.

There are more and more churches that are taking major green steps that can only be a good thing for the church as well as the congregation and its adherents. The cynics among us may be surprised, but as these eco-conscious churches prove, worshipers in the new millennium are willing to put their money into caring for God's creation. The designers, builders and members of these churches have created a new paradigm for congregations worldwide, modeling respect for the planet's natural resources and placing the goal of environmentalism up there with the virtues of purity and piety

Keystone Community Church of Grand Rapids, Mich., the first LEED-certified church in the country, was completed in August 2004. The building sits on a 35-acre site with rolling hills, heavy woods and wetlands, providing a beautiful backdrop to a glass curtain wall and a barrier against harsh winter winds. The natural materials, clear windows redefine the traditional church atmosphere. Likewise, the building sets a new standard for luxury in the form of natural light, fresh air and wide-open spaces.

Green Castle Baptist Church has always been green in name, but not in paradigm. When the congregation outgrew its old building several years ago, the group made a commitment to build a new eco-friendly church. The newly built church in Louisville, Ky., has high-efficiency utilities, zone-controlled spaces and a special film on windows to reduce cooling needs in summer. Green Castle Baptist is the first Energy Star church in Kentucky.

Delaney Hall at Emerson's Unitarian Universalist Church in Houston, Texas, was designed with a goal of being lean and green. The result is a building that is more than 30 percent more efficient than standard buildings, earning Emerson an estimated savings of more than $12,000 annually. During the construction process, stringent indoor air quality standards were met and a significant amount of construction and demolition waste was recycled. The landscape design uses native plants to conserve water, attract wildlife and provide opportunities for environmental learning. Emerson also purchased a 50 percent carbon offset, totaling 185,975 kilowatt hours.

In San Rafael, Calif., the Dominican Sisters' House of Formation is an idyllic campus designed for green and sustainable living that was certified Gold by the LEED rating system. Surrounding a meditative garden full of drought-tolerant and native species, the building is situated to maximize sun exposure for rooftop solar panels. A solar hot water heating system and photovoltaic solar panels provide additional energy savings. Much of the cabinets, carpet, insulation, floors, paints and other building supplies are recycled or reclaimed.

Bridge of Allan Church is one of more than 180 eco-congregations in Scotland making the commitment to tackle climate change. This sustainably built church utilizes radiators connected to a ground source heat pump and under floor heating.

It is encouraging to see these inroads of environmental consciousness into the conservative arena. In the next section of this book I will deal with the Biblical mandate for environmentalism.

My concern is genuine and my perspective is from what may be described as an ultra-conservative viewpoint. I hope that readers will begin to understand why some conservatives allow political alliances to override common sense. This is not a "hall pass" for anyone who does not live sustainably but rather it is intended to be an insightful look into why environmental consciousness is such a one-sided effort.

Ben Thomas

CHAPTER 11

"In the beginning God Created the heaven and the earth."

— Genesis 1:1 —

INROADS TO THE RIGHT

BIBLICAL MANDATE FOR ENVIRONMENTALISM

In the final chapters of this book I will share my personal journey as an evangelical Christian to becoming the environmentalist that I am today. I have not "arrived" yet but welcome scrutiny and challenges by my eco-conscious friends to take more steps toward a darker shade of green.

In the following pages I wish to share my personal Bible-based beliefs on God's mandate for environmentalism. I am not ashamed of my personal beliefs — they provide a foundation of strength for my spirit. I will not apologize for what I believe by my faith in God. Because I believe in a literal interpretation of the Bible as the inspired and Holy Word of God I am impervious to criticism from non-believers. The reason for my security in what I believe and to understand why some of my friends don't "get it" is summed up in I Corinthians 2:14-15 (the following is from The Message). "The unspiritual self, just as it is by nature, can't receive the gifts of God's Spirit. There's no capacity for them. They seem like so much silliness. Spirit can be known only by spirit — God's Spirit and our spirits in open communion. Spiritually alive, we have access to everything God's Spirit is doing, and can't be judged by unspiritual critics."

Psalm 8 says "When I consider Your heavens, the work of your fingers, the moon and the stars which You have ordained. What is man that You are mindful of him... You have crowned him with glory and honor. You have made him to have dominion over the works of Your hands; You have put all things under his feet." (vs. 3-6 / NKJV) These verses offer an absolute directive for man to assume the responsibility for the earth — for all of creation. This chapter leaves no doubt that failure to be eco-conscious is disobedience to God.

God wants us to take care of His creation. Genesis 2:15 says that the Lord put man in the Garden of Eden to work it and take care of it. He followed this with His original plan for mankind to have a vegan diet— of every tree of the garden you may eat. No plans for a slaughter house— cultivate the land and eat the fruit of your labors. If you've ever been to a church pot-luck dinner you know that a lot of Christians are in big trouble!

God saw that the light was good, and he separated the light from the darkness. (Genesis 1:4) God called the dry ground "land," and the gathered waters he called "seas." And God saw that it was good. (Genesis 1:10) The land produced vegetation: plants bearing seed according to their kinds and trees bearing fruit with seed in it according to their kinds. And God saw that it was good. (Genesis 1:12) to govern the day and the night, and to separate light from darkness. And God saw that it was good. (Genesis 1:18) So God created the great creatures of the sea and every living and moving thing with which the water teems, according to their kinds, and every winged bird according to its kind. And God saw that it was good. (Genesis 1:21) God made the wild animals according to their kinds, the livestock according to their kinds, and all the creatures that move along the ground according to their kinds. And God saw that it was good. (Genesis 1:25)

The earth is the Lord's, and everything in it, the world, and all who live in it. (Psalm 24:1) for, "The earth is the Lord's, and everything in it." (1 Corinthians 10:26) For the creationist evangelical there is nothing so sacred as the Words of God. Nonetheless, there seems to be nothing so unimportant as following the mandate to care for that creation. Christians who ignore the first words of the canonical scriptures would do well to take stock and lead by example.

God made it clear in His Word that He feeds the birds of the air, displaying his care for them. "Look at the birds of the air; they do not sow or reap or store away in barns, and yet your heavenly Father

97

feeds them. Are you not much more valuable than they?" (Matthew 6:26) "Consider the ravens: They do not sow or reap, they have no storeroom or barn; yet God feeds them. And how much more valuable you are than birds!" (Luke 12:24) "Aren't two sparrows sold for a small coin? But not one of them will fall to the ground without your Father knowing about it already." (Matthew 10:29) The lesson here is that he cares for nature in a loving way, and we are His most important part of the creation. He tells us that He came to earth to save us — but still, not even one bird falls without His knowledge. The inference in these Scriptures is that we are to do His work on earth—care for all nature.

It is not only the birds for which He cares. There is a progression in Psalm 8:6-8 from "flocks and herds" who are domesticated animals to "all that swim in the sea," which are creatures that most people have never seen. Furthermore, the dominion with which He entrusts us is a gift, not a right.

Dominion does not mean that we can do anything we want with God's creation. The bookend verses 1 and 9 of this chapter use two different words for God. The first *Lord* refers to *Yahweh*, God's personal name but verse 9 is the Hebrew word *Adonai*, which means ruler or *sovereign*. This is a reminder of how God's dominion over us affects our dominion over His creation. We are to approach nature with nurture and care and to be conscious of our God-given responsibilities.

It is incumbent upon me to follow the line of thought, for herein lies the heart of the matter for evangelical Christian environmentalism. I would like to see a movement of eco-consciousness begin to grow and spread among believers today. I almost said "start" among believers; but obviously this movement *was started* millennia ago by God Himself as recorded in the Pentateuch by Moses.

Regarding those who Christians believe to be the first humans, Adam and Eve, Genesis 1:28 says "And God blessed them, and God said to them, Be fruitful, and multiply, and replenish the earth, and subdue it and have *dominion* over the fish of the sea, and over the fowl of the air, and *over every living thing* that moves upon the earth." There, once more: "dominion … over every living thing."

Just as Christians believe that Christ did not come to earth as "king" we must look at His type dominion in the context of leading by serving others; and in His case the others would be *every living thing.* When comparing the Old Testament with the New Testament there are parallels so striking as to be conclusive in their impact.

King David of Israel wrote in Psalm 104: 10-28 about the thoroughness of God's care over nature. He no doubt observed many of the things about which he wrote not only when he was King, but also when he was a shepherd body on the hillsides of Judea. God called a boy who had dominion over a flock of sheep and prepared him to have dominion over his people. With that in mind, consider how environmentalists, whatever their beliefs, should take the lead in caring for every living thing on earth.

Here are the verses from Psalm 104:10-28 that show David's understanding of God's oneness with nature. "He makes springs pour water into the ravines; it flows between the mountains. They give water to all the beasts of the field; the wild donkeys quench their thirst. The birds of the air nest by the waters; they sing among the branches. He waters the mountains from his upper chambers; the earth is satisfied by the fruit of his work. He makes grass grow for the cattle, and plants for man to cultivate-- bringing forth food from the earth: wine that gladdens the heart of man, oil to make his face shine, and bread that sustains his heart. The trees of the LORD are well watered, the cedars of Lebanon that he planted. There the birds make their nests; the stork has its home in the pine trees. The high mountains belong to the wild goats; the crags are a refuge for the rabbits. The moon marks off the seasons, and the sun knows when to go down. You bring darkness, it becomes night, and all the beasts of the forest prowl. The lions roar for their prey and seek their food from God. The sun rises, and they steal away; they return and lie down in their dens. Then man goes out to his work, to his labor until evening. How many are your works, O LORD! In wisdom you made them all; the earth is full of your creatures. There is the sea, vast and spacious, teeming with creatures beyond number-- living things both large and small. There the ships go to and fro, and the leviathan, which you formed to frolic there. These all look to you to give them their food at the proper time. When you give it to them, they gather it up; when you open your hand, they are satisfied with good things." (Psalm 104:10-28)

Just as King David saw God, and as Christians see His Son, Jesus Christ as our Shepherd. , II Samuel 5:1-3 sums it up for us: "He (God) chose David His servant and took him from the sheep pens; from tending the sheep he brought him to be the shepherd of his people Jacob, of Israel his inheritance. And David shepherded them with integrity of heart; with skillful hands he led them."

If this is our example, then what is our excuse for our performance thus far? Believers (i.e. evangelical Christians, Catholics, Jews, any one who believes in God) have been given dominion as a priceless and important trust. If we do not obey His commands, we sin and fail our God. Too many church leaders spend their lives in sanctimonious and hypocritical brow-beating and brain-washing of their flock (congregations/assembly) about every nut and bolt of theological dogma and pharisaical separatist lifestyle choice that they miss God's first great point: He made the earth and gave man kind *dominion* over it..

Ezekiel the prophet gave a warning to shepherd leaders who only took care of themselves in Ezekiel chapter 34 when he said "Should not shepherds take care of the flock? You eat the curds, clothe yourselves with the wool and slaughter the choice animals, but you do not take care of the flock."

The prophet Isaiah 40:11, the prophet remarked about the Sovereign Lord coming with power: " He tends his flock like a shepherd; He gathers them under his arms and carries them close to His heart; He gently leads those that have young." Christ's words are recorded by the John in John 10:11: "I am the good shepherd, The good shepherd lays down his life for the sheep."

Even in the last book of the Bible, Revelation, God makes it perfectly clear about the status of those who destroy His creation. "The nations were angry; and your wrath has come. The time has come for judging the dead, and for rewarding your servants the prophets and your saints and those who reverence your name, both small and great— and for destroying those who destroy the earth." (Revelation 11:18)

Because of their large numbers, American evangelicals could be a critical component of the burgeoning eco-religious movement. About 60 million Americans identify as evangelical Protestants. Energy Star estimates that if each of the more than 300,000 houses of worship in the United States cut energy consumption by 10 percent, congregations would save $200 million.

"American society is in a culture war. Some groups believe the Earth was created 10,000 years ago, the others, 4.5 billion. Getting people of faith concerned and on the same side about environment is a big part of that."

Some religious leaders hope the environmental movement might change the demographics of religious institutions, bringing in young people who care about the environment on a spiritual level.

More things that the Bible says about the earth, God's creation:

Psalms 104: 25-30 - There is the sea, vast and spacious, teeming with creatures beyond number— living things both large and small. There the ships go to and fro, and the leviathan, which you formed to frolic there. These all look to you to give them their food at the proper time. When you give it to them, they gather it up; when you open your hand, they are satisfied with good things. When you hide your face, they are terrified; when you take away their breath, they die and return to the dust. When you send your Spirit, they are created, and you renew the face of the earth. (NIV)

Colossians 1:16-17 - For by him all things were created: things in heaven and on earth, visible and invisible, whether thrones or powers or rulers or authorities; all things were created by him and for him. He is before all things, and in him all things hold to-gether. (NIV)

Nehemiah 9:6 - You alone are the LORD. You made the heavens, even the highest heavens, and all their starry host, the earth and all that is on it, the seas and all that is in them. You give life to everything, and the multitudes of heaven worship you. (NIV)

Isaiah 24:4-6 - The earth dries up and withers, the world languishes and withers, the exalted of the earth languish. The earth is defiled by its people; they have disobeyed the laws, violated the statutes and broken the everlasting covenant. Therefore a curse consumes the earth; its people must bear their guilt. Therefore earth's inhabitants are burned up, and very few are left. (NIV)

Ben Thomas

WORLD NEIGHBORS

THE SECOND, THIRD, & FOURTH
MOST NUMEROUS RELISIONS ON EARTH

Sustainable Me II

ISLAM
HINDUSIM
BUDDHISM

CHAPTER 12

"Do not cause corruption on the earth."
— Quran 2:11 —

WORLD NEIGHBORS

ISLAM

What does the Quran say about our environment? Unfortunately, as Americans we are taught that everyone is our enemy and that there is non common ground. There is common ground on many fronts, not the lest of which is environmentalism.

Quran urges Muslims:

♦ Not to spoil the environment,
♦ To plant trees and spread the green,
♦ Condemns those who spoil the earth

Following are some quotes from the Quran

The Quran says much about the environment... in brief: humans are guardians of God's Creation (Quran 6:165), and we should not create disorder/ pollution (Quran 30:40) - especially as Quran/ Islam came to humanity, not just this generation for us to use to our heart's content. Only humans need the guidance of a scripture as only the human species has a free will; all other species do their God given task automatically (e.g. bees pollinating flowers). Note this does not make us superior and thus allow us to abuse, as we're all God's species (Quran 6:38). Note the names of so many of the chapters in the Quran after named after elements of the Quran and 1/8 of the verses directly or indirectly talk of the environment/ Creation. This is not a coincidence, but emphasizes importance of issue.

♦ Other significant quotes:

And when it is said to them, "Do not cause corruption on the earth," they say, "We are but reformers." Quran, 2:11

♦ And of the people is he whose speech pleases you in worldly life, and he calls Allah to witness as to what is in his heart, yet he is the fiercest of opponents. And when he goes away, he strives throughout the land to cause corruption therein and destroy crops and animals. And Allah does not like corruption. Quran, chapter 2, 204-205

♦ And cause not corruption upon the earth after its reformation. And invoke Him in fear and aspiration. Indeed, the mercy of Allah is near to the doers of good. Quran, 7:56

♦ But those who break the covenant of Allah after contracting it and sever that which Allah has ordered to be joined and spread corruption on earth - for them is the curse, and they will have the worst home. Quran, chapter 13:25

♦ Corruption has appeared throughout the land and sea by what the hands of people have earned so He may let them taste part of what they have done that perhaps they will return. Quran, 30:41

CHAPTER 13

Earth provides enough to satisfy every man's need, but not every man's greed.

— Mahatma Gandhi —

WORLD NEIGHBORS
HINDUISM

Many of the teachings of the Hindu religion reflect their eco-conscious views. First, they believe that *Life is Sacred*. All living beings are sacred because they are parts of God, and should be treated with respect and compassion. This is because the soul can be reincarnated into any form of life. Hinduism is full of stories that treat animals as divine and most Hindus are vegetarian because of this belief in the sanctity of life. Even trees, rivers and mountains are believed to have souls, and should be cared for.

The *virtue of a simple life* has always been prized in Hindu society. Teachers, or Brahmans, are advised to live on the charity of others and not accumulate too much wealth. The most highly respected person in Hindu society is the sadhu, or sage who lives outside normal society, in forests or caves, or travels on foot from one town to another, living simply and consuming as little as possible.

Hinduism stresses that *true happiness comes from within* not from outer possessions. Life's main purpose is to discover the spiritual nature and the peace and fulfillment it brings.

Hindus revere sacred rivers, mountains, forests and animals, and love to be close to nature. Many Hindu villages have a sacred lake, and around irrigate surrounding fields and supply village wells with drinking water. These lakes and groves are places of tranquility and sanctuaries for wildlife, but in recent times the neglect of these simple techniques for gathering and protecting clean water has led to serious water shortages and advancing desertification in many parts of India.

Hinduism is a remarkably diverse religious and cultural phenomenon, with many local and regional manifestations. Within this universe of beliefs, several important themes emerge. These diverse theologies suggest that Dharma -- often translated as "duty" -- can be reinterpreted to include our responsibility to care for the earth, simple living is a model for the development of sustainable economies, our treatment of nature directly affects our karma.

Gandhi exemplified many of these teachings, and his example continues to inspire contemporary social, religious, and environmental leaders in their efforts to protect the planet.

CHAPTER 14

"The roots of all goodness lie in the soil of appreciation for goodness. "

Dalai Lama

WORLD NEIGHBORS

BUDDHISM

Buddhist say that they really care for the environment; they do not harm any living creature or eat meat— as a rule they are all vegetarians. Buddhists believe people should show Metta, loving kindness to all things. Doing this promotes a person good karma, which makes the environment a better place.

Essentially, according to Buddhist teachings, the ethical and moral principles are governed by examining whether a certain action is likely to be harmful to one's self or to others and thereby avoiding any actions which are likely to be harmful. Very little is taught specifically about the environment other than the precept of respecting all life. This fourth largest religion has not been updated for Eco-consciousness

The five precepts are training rules, which, if one were to break any of them, one should be aware of the breech and examine how such a breech may be avoided in the future. It entails less feelings of guilt than its Judeo-Christian counterpart.

Buddhism places a great emphasis on 'mind' and it is mental anguish such as remorse, anxiety, guilt etc. which is to be avoided in order to cultivate a calm and peaceful mind. The five precepts are:

♦ Avoid taking the life of beings. All beings have a right to their lives and that right should be respected.

♦ Avoid taking things not given. avoid taking anything unless one can be sure that is intended for you.

♦ Avoid sensual misconduct. it covers any overindulgence in any sensual pleasure

♦ Refrain from false speech. avoiding lying, deceiving, slander and speech which is not beneficial to others.

♦ Abstain from substances which cause intoxication and heedlessness. it does not infer any intrinsic evil in, say, alcohol itself but indulgence in such a substance that could be the cause of breaking the other four precepts

ATHEISM (Side Note)

Can an atheist be an environmentalist?

This brief thesis may help to explain why there is (or should be) internal tension for the atheist environmentalist. This does not mean an atheist cannot *be* moral and an environmentalist; of course a person may be both. But it leads us to question where the grounding for such a combination could come from.

On one hand they or we believe that destruction of our natural environment is wrong; not just wrong in the sense of "I don't like it" but in the sense of being objectively *wrong*.

Without (a) God, claiming an objective moral rule loses its grounding because there is nothing (to give it legitimate authority. You lose your grounding: It's like trying to stand firmly on nothing.

If you believe that destroying our Earth is wrong, *really* wrong, this necessitates belief in objective moral values, which in turn necessitates the existence of a God to provide the grounding for moral laws. Think about this.

A FRIST PERSON LOOK AT AN EVANGELICAL CONSERVATIVE JOURNEY OF SUSTAINABILITY

Sustainable Me II

EARLY SUSTAINABILITY

AN UNLIKELY HERITAGE

CHEMICALS COME HOME

GUESS WHO'S COMING TO DINNER

THE SEVERN "R's"

EARTH-BERMED PASSIVE SOLAR HOME

IT ISN'T EASY BEING GREEN

INTO DEEPER SHADES OF GREEN

SUSTAINABLE ME

15: EARLY SUSTAINABILITY

Babies were booming all around the country when I was born in 1947. In fact two of my best friends growing up were Ronnie and Sylvia— second cousins, born that same June —same country church— same schools— same sustainable type households — same kind of loving, sharing parents and families.

Our parents had big gardens, cows for milk and butter, chickens for — ummm — chicken and eggs, hogs for bacon, ham, sausage, lard, and unfortunately chitlins (they are really chittetrlings — but then again folks in my part of the country were never that impressed with putting a "G" on the end of a word). We also all had farm ponds with bass, perch, bream, and catfish.

Along the edge of fields and stream and creek banks grew wild muscadine grapes (red) and black berries. Everyone had a grape arbor for scuppernong grapes and all sorts of fruit trees and bushes; Apple, pear, peach, persimmon and fig. Oh yes, there were nut trees as well—walnut, pecan and in the woods, wild hickory nuts. Growing in the wild were watercress, which were commonly referred to as "creasy greens."

We did not have much money, but imagine being born into this world of plenty. From an early age I was taught how to harvest the delicacies so abundant, the best ways to prepare them to eat, and how to best preserve them for use until the next harvest appeared.

As long ago as I can remember, we had a massive garden .
We were only a family of four (counting my maternal grandfather)
and I just didn't get why my dad thought we needed 4 100' rows of
beans!?! Our garden must have been a good half acre or more with

rows on end of beans, black-eyed peas, crowder peas, tomatoes,
Irish potatoes, cabbage, squash, cucumbers, beets, radish, corn,
pumpkins, peppers, eggplant, collard greens, turnips, onions, and
okra. It was all ours—with extras shared with the neighbors if their
beans "hadn't come in yet" (started producing). Sunday's after
church was one of the best times of sharing in this free farmers'
market of "garden-overabundance."

We were fortunate to live in an area of North Caroline that
bordered on the foothills of the piedmont (red clay and rich loamy
soil) and the Sandhills, sand so deep that the pine trees and peaches
competed for beauty as did watermelon and cantaloupe for mouth-
watering favor in the early summertime.

What did we do with all these organic blessings? We ate
like kings. How did we preserve them for later enjoyment. We used
harsh chemicals—like salt, sugar, pepper, allspice, cinnamon, sage,
rosemary, and thyme, we hung hot pepper up on twine to dry and
dried fruit slices in the sun.

Before I started school my mother had me packing quart
Mason and Ball jars with peach, apple, and pear halves. She took
great pride in starting in the bottom of one corner with a juicy peach

half and then spiraling the halves around with one half in each corner until the last possible peach half was in the top. Once we had a canner full of jars, my mother carefully measured a tablespoon of sugar into each jar and then poured it full of water, put on the lid, screwed on the ring as tightly as possible and proceeded with the canning process. I remember so well after those jars came out of the canner, waiting to hear for each jar to "POP" as the lids sealed, meaning the job was done.

It took me a while to learn how to peel peaches or string and snap beans—but with my skinny little arms and fingers, I was a heck of a "packer." I remember one year that my mother canned 248 quarts of green beans. We had beans at least 5 times each week. The next year my daddy only planted 2 rows of beans.

As an only child I guess I didn't mind the work so much—I used to take great joy in counting the amount of pints and quarts that we canned each year. It was more fun canning jelly—wow — the sweet rewards of that task.

Gathering eggs was an easy and rewarding job—but once in a while, the chickens and roosters had a bit of a problem with you entering their space. Getting pecked or chased by a mad rooster is one thing that gave me nightmares as a kid. But farm fresh eggs were so worth the effort. Occasionally a chicken would be protective and "nest" her eggs, a dozen or more and sit happily on them until they hatched into beautiful yellow chicks. More chickens meant more eggs and more great oven-fried chicken dinners with gravy over steaming hot biscuits.

I remember two cows, Sookie and Brownie. Both tall mixed breeds that gave gallons of warm sweet milk.—as much as a gallon and a half every evening. I remember up to 6 inches of cream rising to the top of a gallon of milk, destined to be churned and formed into beautiful golden molds of butter. I was not good at milking cows — swatting flies with her tail always popped me in the head and then there was the episode of finally getting my pail full of milk. I was very proud until she stepped into it .

When I was around ten I got the only sex lesson my dad ever taught me. We hooked a rope to Brownies harness and walked a mile to cousin Tom's house to breed her. I was admittedly shocked to see his short bull trying to ride Brownie piggy back. I guess it wasn't working so after a little discussion Tom and my dad headed for the pasture. After finally coaxing Brownie into the creek, the bull was allowed to approach again standing on the creek bank. Then I realized that the whole set up was done so that he could "help her make a new calf." My daddy gave Tom $20.00 and we walked home. No one said a word.

I must tell you about the hogs. Nasty, nasty! They were fed mostly table scrap, usually topped by a large bucked full of feed as a supplement. This was poured carefully into a long, narrow trough. There was always water that had been carried to a big tub for the hogs to drink. Since we had no electric pump for running water, it was transported the 150 yards one peck bucket at a time after it was drawn from the well.

The hogs were for meat. Not just ANY meat, but ham, pork chops, bacon, tenderloin, ribs, "side-meat" and "fatback" for seasoning, Also, the head and liver, in fact almost everything including the intestines were use for something. Parts were ground into sausage and seasoned to taste and even the fat was rendered down for lard.

The making of sugar cured ham, or "country ham," which most people outside the south find disgustingly salty and tough was quite a production. A mixture of white and brown sugar, salt, black and red pepper, and a variety of other spices to taste. Hams are rubbed with the mixture until there is some absorption and they are fully coated. They are then wrapped in butcher paper and hung in bags to dry. Butchering is done late in fall and the hams cure all winter. They look moldy and disgusting when they are unwrapped, but if you grew up in the South, you know it's yummy.

Extra potatoes, apples, turnips, pumpkins were stored under the home's crawl space until the succumbed to the first hard freeze.

In short, nothing wasted. As if to mark the end of the gardening season and just before the first frost and the coming hog-butchering my mother canned one final delicacy: "End of the garden soup." OH MY! As if in a race with the weather, my mother would pick the last corn, peas, beans, butter beans, tomatoes, potatoes, squash, onions, okra and anything else that was left. She filled the last of the jars to the brims, added a teaspoon of salt, screwed those lids tight and after appropriate boiling time in the canner, we listened to the last lids of the season pop, pop, pop.

My daddy also taught me a few things until he became very sick when I was 12 with a tropical tubercular illness. This disease had him in the hospital for over 10 months and out of work for a few years. He taught me how to fish— he was a fisherman supreme but I was more of a "catcher-man." If they were biting, I was cool. My dad never seemed happier than when he had his rod and reel in hand and his line in the water. It was sport, but he caught and released more than he took home. As you might expect, we had a lot of southern-fried fish for meals.

My boat fishing with my dad ended one fine summer day when he hook what he call a monster jack fish (Chain pickerel). He had the fish at the boat ready for retrieval when the fish suddenly jumped right in the boat, barring his long rows of sharp teeth right between my feet. The fish was in! I was out! Yes, although is was really afraid of 20 foot deep dark lake water, I felt I owed my feet a chance of survival. Fortunately my daddy released "Mr. Jack" and rescued me. That was also the first time I ever heard daddy swear.

Hunting was daddy's other hobby—a had a odd twist or two as I recall. What was he thinking? For the most part he hunted small game which "they" ate. Eating bunnies and squirrels was not on my diet. But when you are poor and the top of the food chain, you need protein. I did learn how to skin a rabbit and a squirrel—much easier than plucking wet chicken feathers by the way. The strange twist was snake hunting—the moccasins were eating the fish. That would not do, So we took to 5 cell flash lights and went over to the pond — to hunt and kill snakes. It was a terrifying experience but one that I evidently needed to survive. We were successful every time. The fish were glad.

I also learned how to trap. Our farm pond was small with an earth dam about 10 feet wide. One year it was chosen by muskrats for burrowing their homes and nearly destroyed the whole "dam" thing. That's when I learned to trap. I must have caught a dozen or more. Daddy and I skinned those bad boys and sold the pelts for $3-5.00 each. We were rich!

The two most hateful things I learned from my daddy were how to shovel cow manure out of the stable after a long cold winter. How could Brownie do this to us? Had she no feminine skills? I remember the first few shovel's full were between my parenthetical "waauuukkkk-k-k" sounds of potential wretches. But one of our neighbors, Raymond, had a manure spreader which meant that at least we didn't have to fertilize our fields by hand as well.

The second chore I hated was hauling and chopping wood. It wasn't nasty, just back breaking. We had no electric range or forced air heat. All cooking and warming of the house was done by wood stoves.

Living in an area prone to hurricanes, there were always trees in the woods that had been blown over and killed. These drying trees were sawed into the proper lengths, loaded on a wagon or pickup truck and hauled to the woodpile at our house to be split and chopped into firewood. Learning how to swing an axe is a skill let me tell you. It was just backbreaking, but I developed a talent for chopping wood and for keeping a big stack on the front porch where it would stay dry. There was a separate wooden box behind the wood-fueled range so that it would be handy when my mom cooked a meal, which she did three times a day.

With only a hand dug water well, with a bucket and rope that was attached to a windless, we pulled water up for drinking and watering the cow and mule. (We'll discuss the mule later.) Sometimes it was so cold that the peck bucket in the kitchen with the dipper in it would freeze over during the night. I almost fell in the well once. I figured I wanted to climb up the 3 foot high rock sides and look in to see where the water came from—I was about 4 years old. All I really remember after crawling to the edge is hearing my mother's twin sister, Aunt Velma scream, come flying outside through the kitchen's screen door and doing some kind of spread-eagle dive tackle in the knick of time to save me from a deadly fall. Thanks sweetheart.

There are but a few glimpses into our sustainable lifestyle in the 1950's. Obviously be had another word for sustainable, for us it was survival. My parents only had to purchase a few items when they went to town every couple of weeks: Flour, coffee, tea, sugar, salt and spices, soap and necessary hygiene products and maybe an occasional treat when it could be afforded.

16: AN UNLIKELY HERITAGE

This section could be subtitled " The Bully and the Boot-legger" if I were being honest. So, Let's be honest. I had two very unique grandfathers. One, I lived with along with my parents until the day he died. The other was private and remote, but taught me more than he knew.

Granddaddy Thomas was such a bully and I've got to add, a real SOB. Never a kind word and always with the walking cane, which when I was about twelve, came cracking down right on the middle of my forehead. It I hadn't been so hard-headed it would have probably killed me. As I recalled, he felt that I had not re-sponded quickly enough to take is coffee cup to the kitchen for a refill while he sat on his fat a— in his rocking chair.

My mother had talked my daddy into believing that grand-daddy could not survive for long and needed to be cared for. Sure enough, he had a stroke when he was about 70 which proved her point. He was really good at giving orders to everyone because the little wood shack in which we lived was *his* house, not my parents. He constantly was giving orders and I very seldom saw him lift a finger to help. He was the master. For me, growing up in his shad-ow was a nightmare, but he did teach me a couple of things in rare moments that have stuck with me. First, of course, is to never hit anyone in the head with a walking cane—it hurts like heck.

Ben Thomas

Another odd lesson—literally was how to take a dump in the snow. (We had no indoor plumbing—and no outhouse until I was twelve years old.) In a foot of snow, it is difficult to take a proper squat with your forearms crooked behind your knees to keep your balance. He suggested that I find a tree with two horizontal limbs forming a "V" a few feet off the ground. All I had to do then was climb the tree, pull down my pants, hug the tree, make sure that everything was pointed in the downward direction and let it go. If you don't think that if funny then you don't have a sense of humor.

In earlier years Granddaddy Thomas did teach me something more sustainable than how to crap in the snow (biodegradable recycling). One crisp fall day he hitched up old Molly, the mule, to his buckboard style wagon, loaded it with bags of shelled dry corn and I got to go with him to the mill—about a 2 mile drive. When we got there and the wagon was unloaded the grist wheel was engaged to the water coming over the dam and the grinding began. I got to watch. I can still remember the corn going into a hopper and watching with fascination as the grinding began. There was some discussion among the men there and my granddaddy clarified that he wanted about 2 toe bags (burlap gunny sacks) of cornmeal, a finer grind and the rest was to be a coarse grind for livestock feed during the winter. Old Molly sweated a lot on that mile long hill up from the millpond to the church, but after that it was mostly downhill back home. The cornbread was great, the pigs squealed and grunted and the cow slobbered enthusiastically when they got a taste of their freshly ground meal. Molly, well she had hers as well as a long cool drink of water. Now, that is what is called homesteading sustainability.

One year we planted about an acre of sorghum. We watched it grow and I thought it was really tasty when I was given a stem to suck on. It was like sugar candy. I little sinewy but oh so sweet. Then one day, it was all cut down and taken to the sorghum mill. There it was processed and made into something called black strap molasses. I imitated my granddaddy as he poured a big puddle of the molasses onto his plate, sliced off a huge chunk of warm butter and stirred them together with his fork. Then— the hot steaming biscuit was dipped into that mixture and sopped up like gravy. I followed suit and was in molasses heaven. Again, very sustainable processes as the tops of the sorghum and leaves became fodder for the livestock. And a good, sweet time was had by all!

I guess he was a motivator as well. Granddaddy kept after my mother to make some kraut, or can some apples, or make apple sauce, or pick some blackberries, or he saw some grapes down by the creek and took the ladder down so she "could get to 'em easy." Or, he would say "You need to feed that milk to the hogs—seems like Brownie got into them wild onions again and it ain't fit for drinkin'." He was an observant man and living in his house kept me in touch will all my cousins. We all turned out well in spite of granddaddy's "charms" and I'm proud to be a part of the family.

Now, Grandpa Cole was different. A bit more successful and a harder worker. He raised nine children through the depression the hard way. During the early years he actually ran the mill that ground everyone's corn, wheat, and rye into meal and flour. During World War II my dad sent home most of his money to help Grandpa Cole buy a nice farm where he could made more money and even buy a Ford Model T.

Fortunately, Grandpa Cole was MUCH more bio-diversified than a lot of men with nine children. My parents never told me this, but one night I was told by a boyhood friend of my dad's, Roy Williams. Roy said, "You know something, a thought a lot of your daddy when we were growing up, in fact we lived up the hill right across the creek from the mill pond. I liked your grandpa too although a lot of people didn't like him making that moonshine. But, hell, what was a man with nine children going to do to feed them during the depression?" You could have knocked me over with a feather! My grandpa, a bootlegger?

That was a Saturday night so I chose my opportunity to ask my parents about it at Sunday dinner the next day. I knew it was true when my mother dropped that big plate of golden brown, hot, steaming biscuits and they fell, as if in embarrassed slow motion, one by one to the dining room floor. In todays vernacular, "OMG!" My mother apologized, and said something about hoping I would never have to know the truth. My wife kicked me under the table. My eldest, at five, said "Daddy, what's a bootlegger? Are we going to have to go to hell?"

I said "No son, but you had a very clever great grandpa."

Clever he was. I *had* been told several times how grandpa Cole had been arrested by the township constable who happened to ride by the house up the hill from the mill and caught grandpa playing his banjo on the front porch on a Sunday. Seems he had been caught for an alleged law about "breaking the Sabbath." Do you sense shades of Al Capone here?

Can't find the still, can't catch him selling "shine," can't find anyone to testify against him in court — but dang it all, he's done disturbed the quiet of a Sunday afternoon. It's such an amusing tale. In fact, I just went to BevMo and bought a quart of corn liquor in his honor when I started writing this section of the book.

Back to organic farming and bio-fuels now. Seems as how I remember my daddy telling me that that old Model-T could use almost anything for fuel including, gas, kerosene, and even "likker." Corn was a cash crop then as well as today. (Now if they would just stop ruining it with GMOs, pesticides, insecticides, just help us end our dependence on fossil fuels!

Just to be clear, moonshine was not his only talent—he was quite adept at apple cider and wine. All organic and potent. I remember my dad telling me that he and his only two sisters as small children found the jugs of wine and decided to have a party. They found them all passed out on the grain floor in the barn several hours later. I'm not sure if it was the wine or perhaps some "corn squzzin's", but a good time was had by all, I'm sure.

One more thing Grandpa Cole showed me how to do—that I'm only picked up on in recent years. Prior to that I was more like granddaddy Thomas: I had to argue and there was no question that I was always right ... about everything. When Grandma Cole started in on Grandpa and wanted to fuss or argue, he would stand up out of his rocking chair by the window, walk right past her rocker, down the hall to the kitchen and out the back door without a word. Funny— she would still be talking as if he were there. Sometimes we would all do well to quietly walk away from an argument—say over sustainability or environmental issues— and then kindly and thoughtfully talk it through later.

They were intelligent men born in the wrong place and at the wrong time to have a chance to be successful by the world's terms. But I do believe that the bootlegger and the bully could have very well been the bio-chemist and the businessman instead. They did encourage their children to be successful and they all were, in their chosen fields of occupation. And the descendants on both sides of the family are bankers, businessmen, doctors, lawyers, school administrators, teachers, bio-chemists, law enforcement officials, artists, manufacturers, and I for one a very proud to be related to each of them—even the ones that piss me off occasionally.

Here is to my family and yours: May we love each other, learn from each other, and when needed, lend one another a hand.

The Still

Grandpa had a super idea— he even used it in his Ford Model-T. Looks like we took an expensive detour.

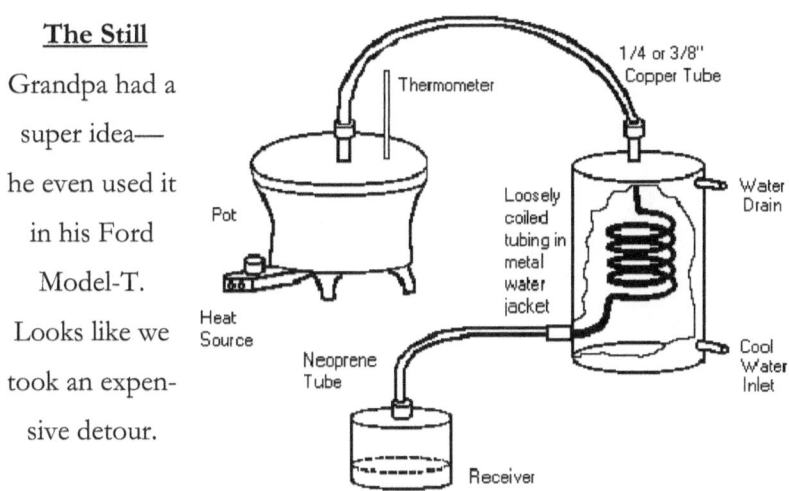

Corn ethanol is produced by means of ethanol fermentation and distillation; a sophisticated modern version of a "moonshine" still. Taking a sip from a modern car's fuel tank is a bad idea. The petroleum-based fuels that power most of the world's automobiles are far removed from anything safe to drink.

But that's changing. A growing industry has been investigating fossil-fuel alternatives for decades, and much of their research focuses on biofuels -- petroleum substitutes made from natural plant oils. Rudolph Diesel originally designed the engine that bears his name in an attempt to give farmers the ability to operate equipment using locally grown fuel.

Some plants, such as corn, contain sugars that, when fermented like beer and liquor, produce ethanol, an alcohol that can be used as fuel.

17: CHEMICALS COME HOME

When the 60's had rolled around I had been working for neighborhood farmers for 6 years—since the second grade. I was always glad to made the 50 cents an hour I could make as a child. I worked for peach and tobacco farmers and it was more like play for me, an only child, to be around other children for hours on end.

By the time I was entering high school, I was a field hand, not just a barn helper. Also I was selective and worked for the Thompson family, the Blakeley's, and the Rushing's who paid me a whooping $1.25 per hour plus morning and afternoon breaks. Of course I worked for my best friend's dad, Raymond who paid me at the end of the season in one lump sum. I wouldn't have liked that from anyone else, but it worked well—one big fat handful of money—it was like a bank to me. I also worked for Homer who was a neighbor and "put it" (harvested the tobacco, and "put it in" the barn for curing) on the same day as Raymond. Homer was to pay at season's end as well, but for the record, he never paid me a dime. After three years I took my Saturday's elsewhere and was paid.

Now that's the good part of the story. A young boy earning enough to buy all his school clothes and even a transistor radio and cassette recorder later on. I was a player for sure.

After a busy day in the tobacco fields we would be covered in tar. Not even lava soap would clean it off. What do you think we used to clean off tar? Out to the garden we'd go and grab the ripest big tomato that we could find and crush it in our hands. Away went the tar: Another organic cleanser located! But something else started happening. Kids were getting sick—nauseated, fevers and chills, vomiting.

I noticed that in the early mornings when the tobacco was heavy with due and we would all get wet from bending over to harvest the lower leaves many of the boys would get sick and vomit. Mr. Bud Thompson used to pay me to "top" his tobacco plants and pull suckers—guess he was the only farmer who didn't have a son to do it for free. Then, one year no one had to pull suckers from the top of each leaf or to top the plants.

Tobacco produces a single stalk with a terminal bud at the top. The bud exhibits large blooms. At each leaf lateral buds may be produced. Removal of the tops along with the removal or restriction of sucker growth results in certain desirable changes in the cured leaf such as: increased root growth and support of the growth and development of upper leaves. Increased root growth means an increase in the potential for uptake of water and nutrients, increased support for the upper plant against wind, and an increase in the plant's potential to synthesize nicotine.

Chemical topping would appear to be the ideal method for eliminating the production of excess leaves and the top which will flower while chemical Contacts and Systemics are methods of chemical sucker control. Maleic hydrazide (MH) is the systemic used, a toxin which is regulated by the EPA, yet aids in the synthesis of nicotine. Chemicals on tobacco is but one example of the post world war two chemical invasion into our lives. Some parents made their children stop working in tobacco when the random sicknesses began.

DDT (dichlorodiphenyltrichloroethane) is an insecticide which is a colorless, crystalline solid, tasteless and almost odorless chemical compound. The Swiss chemist Paul Hermann Müller was awarded the Nobel Prize in Medicine in 1948 for his discovery of the high efficiency of DDT as a contact poison against several arthropods. After the war, DDT was made available for use as an agricultural insecticide, and its production and use increased. The success of its use was not lost on the Southern farmer, who found using DDT and other chemicals saved time and made them money.

Silent Spring by American biologist Rachel Carson was published in 1962. The book catalogued the environmental impacts of spraying DDT and questioned the logic of releasing large amounts of chemicals into the environment without fully understanding their effects on ecology or human health. I recall that farmers and even school teachers resented the book being placed in libraries because of some "crazy woman's" fantasies.

Its publication was one of the signature events in the birth of the environmental movement, and resulted in a large public outcry that eventually led to DDT being banned for agricultural use in the US in 1972. DDT was subsequently banned for agricultural use worldwide under the Stockholm Convention.

Carbaryl used chiefly as an insecticide commonly sold under the brand name **Sevin**, a trademark of the Bayer Company. It remains the third most-used insecticide in the United States for home gardens, commercial agriculture, and forestry and rangeland protection. Although toxic to insects, carbaryl is detoxified and eliminated rapidly in vertebrates. It is neither concentrated in fat nor secreted in the milk. For the latter reasons, carbaryl is favored for food crops, at least in the US. It is the active ingredient in Carylderm shampoo used to combat head lice until infestation is eliminated. The production of carbaryl caused the Bhopal disaster, in India, the largest industrial accident in history. This accident caused around 11,000 deaths and over 500,000 injuries. It is classified as a likely human carcinogen by the United States Environmental Protection Agency.

At this point it would be good for you to refer back to chapter nine of this book; TOXINS: Insecticides and Pesticides. More than the flower topping and sucker control in the fields where I worked — more than the Sevin dust I helped put on our garden to control pests on beans, peas, tomatoes and potatoes — more than herbicides and pesticides — we were being infected with a host of World War II chemicals which should have outlived their usefulness. And guess who moved into the neighborhood—killer toxins, DDT, carcinogens?

And, unknown to me, in farms in the Midwest, citrus groves in the south and west, cranberry farms in the north east, and potatoes in the northwest, chemicals were being invited into those neighborhoods as well. These new visitors were seen to be our helper, our way to bigger, better crops and yields. Regardless of the great wake up call by _Silent Spring,_ few were willing to heed the warning and demand answers.

The age of the organic farmer had disappeared from our midst. We were happy not to have insects, pests, and nutrient sucking plant appendages pulling away our crop dollars. We were living in a modern world.

Whether it is chemical use on a farm, preservatives in packaged produce, or discoveries in medicine, we should be vigilant and make sure that the cure is not worse than the current methods.

18: GUESS WHO'S COMING TO DINNER ?

Innovation and corporate greed answered the call of con-venience and two-income households. Consumers wanted more, and an easier life. Time was consumed with more activities which meant less time to work in the garden and to preserve food. We had new friends to invited to dinner.

Beginning in the 1950's, spurred in part by the success of World War II C Rations' success, canned foods and other conven-ient packaging began to become the norm for family dinner.

C Rations were individual canned, pre-cooked, and prepared wet ration. It was intended to be issued to U.S. military land forces when fresh food (packaged unprepared food prepared in mess halls or field kitchens was impractical or not available. Operational condi-tions often caused the C-ration to be standardized for field issue re-gardless of environmental suitability or weight limitations.

Corporate America seized upon consumers' desire to have the food they wanted ready to eat in a quick preparation time with-out the bother of a lot of hands on activity. People could have a huge variety of food products from around the world, in season and out, and have it when they wanted it. Heck, they didn't even realize it wasn't very good and that there were dozens of toxic chemicals in every can and wrapper.

Let's have a dinner party and just look who's on the guest list! The first in line is refined sugar. High consumption of sugar, and the corresponding elevated insulin levels, can cause weight gain, bloating, fatigue, arthritis, migraines, lowered immune function, gallstones, obesity, breast cancer, gum disease and cavities, and cardiovascular disease. Aren't you glad that little sweetie is on the list. Honey couldn't come and molasses was just a bit old fashioned.

Our next guest is a slick and ruthless guy: Partially Hydrogenated Vegetable Oil. It is made by reacting vegetable oil with hydrogen. When this occurs, the level of polyunsaturated oils (good fat) is reduced and trans fats are created. Trans fats can be found in foods such as vegetable shortening, some margarines, crackers, candies, baked goods, cookies, snack foods, fried foods, salad dressings, and many processed foods. They are associated with heart disease, breast and colon cancer, atherosclerosis and elevated cholesterol.

Sodium Nitrate and Nitrite are preservatives that are added to canned foods, processed foods and processed meat products such as bacon, corned beef, ham, hot dogs, lunch meats, and sausage. This multi-cultural cross dresser is one of the hits of the party.

MSG, Monosodium Glutamate, is used to flavor food, since food no longer has real flavor because of over cooking, a variety of chemicals and pesticides used and lack of any nutrients left in over farmed soil. MSG destroys nerve cells in the brain but authorities do not seem to care much since it may be hidden in infant formula, low fat milk, candy, chewing gum, drinks, over-the-counter medications.

(especially children's), as a binder and filler for nutritional supplements and fruit yogurts, in prescription drugs, IV fluids given in hospitals, and in the chicken pox vaccine. Lovely, no? But that's not all. This stuff is harmful because, it inhabits natural growth hormone and dramatically promotes irreversible obesity. Other reactions include headaches, nausea, weakness, a burning sensation in the back of neck and forearms, wheezing or difficulty in breathing, and changes in heart rate, pulse rate, and/or heart palpitation. Every dinner has to have that one guest that just gets under everyone's skin—some opinionated old fossil who just loves to meddle — welcome Ms. G. (MSG)

And you must have that cool, suave and debonair devil who's name is on everyone's lips. We just can't get enough of this guy as he slips among the crowd. Who needs that old sour puss lemon or that hot headed tea when we have soft drinks. Soft drinks have artificial sweeteners (Saccharin, NutraSweet, Aspartame) that are small quantities of poison because these alter brain neurochemistry. These drinks also have high fructose corn syrup that has mercury and over time damages body cells.

Another group of guests who always seem to be on the list are the cousins from the "Cide" side of the family. You actually know them, There is Herbi-Cide, Insecti-Cide, and of course Pesti-Cide. This sneaky group just blend in practically unnoticed. They are absorbed by the freshest of vegetables and fruits and are so prevalent that they even find their way into mothers' own milk via the foods we eat. This family is really a group of brats who just can't be trusted.

Our dinner list got a lot longer while I was growing up. In fact, there were so many of these unwanted guests that we just started calling them by their initials: GMO, BHA, BHT, and BVO. Genetically Modified Organisms, BHA/BHT (used and reheated cooking oils), and Brominated Vegetable Oil which is used to keep flavor oils in soft drinks in suspension. Bromate is a poison and reduces immune defenses and depletes histamine, which can lead to allergic reactions.

Admittedly, my dinner guest parody is a departure from my sustainable life journey. But on the other hand, it completely illustrates how subtle the introduction of toxins has been invited into our lives. One minute we are eating a healthy diet, grown organically without the use of toxins, growth inhibitors, or pesticides — then the next we are eating convenient foods. We are enjoying canned foods, frozen food, TV dinners, foods with flavor and color enhancements and very few people even had a passing thought that these might be bad for us.

I'm closing this chapter with a list of toxins and additives that no one should take into their bodies or offer to another:

◆ Acesulfame Potassium. Artificial sweetener: Chewing gum, diet soda, no-sugar added baked goods and desserts, tabletop sweetener (Sunett).

◆ Aspartame (NutraSweet). Artificial sweetener: Frozen desserts, diet soda, tabletop Sweetener (Equal).

- Butylated Hydroxyanisole (BHA). Antioxidant: Cereal packages, chewing gum, oil, potato chips.

- Green 3. Beverages, candy.

- Blue 1. Baked goods, beverages, candy.

- Blue 2. Beverages, candy, pet food.

- Red 3. Baked goods, candy, cherries in fruit cocktail

- Yellow 6. Baked goods, beverages, candy, gelatin, sausage.

- Olestra (Olean). Fat substitute: Lay's Light chips, Pringles Light chips.

- Partially Hydrogenated Oil.   Fat: Baked goods, fried restaurant food, icing, microwave popcorn, pie crust, shortening,, stick margarine.

- Potassium Bromate. Dough strengthener: White flour.

- Propyl Gallate. Antioxidant, preservative: Chewing gum, chicken soup base, meat, potato sticks, oil.

- Saccharin. Artificial sweetener: No-sugar-added foods, tabletop sweetener (Sweet'N Low).

- Sodium Nitrate, Sodium Nitrite. Coloring, flavoring, preservative

- Bacon, corned beef, frankfurters, ham, luncheon meat, smoked fish.

- Stevia. Natural sweetener: Dietary supplement.

19: THE SEVEN R'S

As a young man I studied attended college and earned a Bachelor of Science in secondary education. When I graduated a put my degree to work teaching Civics and World Geography in a high school near my home. Meanwhile my home church planned to open a private Christian school and asked for my help.

This was a leap of faith for both the church and me. We quickly realized that this effort was going to take a lot more work and funds than we had. There was never a thought of not fulfilling that purpose. We did finish the classroom building but there was a matter of furniture, books, and supplies.

We didn't call it sustainability, but we began to search for what we needed. First of all, desks, chairs, tables and books. Oddly enough we found most of these items in Raleigh, the state capitol in a warehouse stacked full of old, used school supplies sold at a very cheap price. Recycle — Reuse. Things were beginning to happen for us even though we did have to buy blackboards. The bulletin board problem was harder to solve. We couldn't afford to buy a couple for each of the class rooms. Then someone suggested that the use 4x8 foot Celotex® ceiling panels. They were cheap, lightweight, and would do the job— we had solved another problem by Reducing our needs.

What a predicament. We had a building, desks, books, bulletin boards and "new" chalk boards. It was 1970 and we are on the verge of a new frontier. Just a couple of problems. Someone had stolen all our doors and door hardware for the building, we only had cinderblock walls, no ceilings and the shingles weren't on the roof.

I finished nailing on the roof shingles myself and we started school with no doors and no ceilings. I remember having students go to the bathrooms in pairs so that one could stand in the hall as a warning guard. We raised money for the doors and ceiling by every means possible. We sold candy, magazine subscriptions, and collected soft drink bottles to redeem at local markets— thousands and thousands of them. Remember when soft drinks came in a glass bottle that you could redeem? That's the way we started Big Oak Christian Academy.

Our penchant for conserving had just begun. There were the other four R's that we had to focus on for our grand total of 19 students on opening day: Reading, 'Riting, 'Rithmetic, and Religion. What a joy as we recycled children from small towns and country farms into scholars that first difficult year. Our Reusing, Recycling, and Reducing continued.

By the second year with 99 students on opening day we did have doors and ceilings—it was beginning to look complete. Teachers discussed ways to save, someone suggested that instead of wasting rolled paper to cover bulletin boards that we buy cheap cotton material that could be reused and shared to cover the boards. Great savings!

In later years our school grew to 250 students and added grades 7-12. We always needed more than we could afford but in some way or another our prayers were answered. We were given the opportunity to tear down some brick walls of an old building if we could use them Leslie Kellam said. So we knocked down the walls and we gathered together and stacked bricks until our hands bled through our gloves

The new elementary building needed carpeting on those bare concrete floors. What could we do? We were fund-raising to pay for the building itself and more recycled desks and chairs. Thank fully a new school parent had an idea. J.B. Short owned a flooring company and offered to give us all the carpet color samples we could use to cover the 6500 square foot floor. We hauled several truck loads of carpet squares and covered all the classroom floors with patterns of every color, thickness, and texture imaginable. It was the '70s— The kids thought they were at a disco every day. It was colorful, it was free, and it was saved from the county landfill.

We recycled and reused a lot of things through the years. From three school closings we were able to scavenge "real" bulletin boards, more desks, book shelves, a cafeteria serving table, sinks, a 15x60 foot velvet curtain for the stage in our gym-torium. Even, glass backboards for our new gym.

With an operable curtain and stage we presented great dra-ma—for real. Where do you suppose we rented our costumes? We didn't. We collected recycled clothing from family and friends of the school and enlisted the help of parents, teachers, and students to remake these into some of the most fantastic costumes you' could ever imagine.

Thanks again to all those who made it possible. I wish that I could mention every name. Those country kids did become scholars and through some 19 years over 90% of the graduates went on to further their education or become a part of the armed forces.

20: Earth-Bermed, Passive Solar Home

In 1982 my wife and I had an opportunity to build a new home. Our first home was a large two-story with electric baseboard heat. During the winter months the electric bill was more than the house payment. In the summer, with no air conditioning it was always hot and muggy. We decided that our new home would be smaller and easier to heat and cool.

During our search for house plans I came across the most interesting magazine called _Mother Earth News._ The intriguing articles in this publication were of earth-bermed homes and passive solar heating. I was fascinated at what I read and the concepts presented. Let me assure you that the search for additional information was a nightmare. Of course there were no search engines—not even an internet. My calls and visits to a number of libraries as well as searches through bookstores on these topics yielded little.

As I discussed Earth-bermed homes and passive solar heat with friends and asked contractors and anyone who would listen, I discovered a few such structures within a 50 mile radius of our land. We visited and were both amazed and frightened at the prospects. I remember one home that the owners were so proud of because they had made a cave complete with a grass lawn on the top. No passive solar but definitely a lot of earth was involved. They even showed my wife and I their air conditioning for days when the temperature was over 90.

They had a big chest type food freezer where they kept gallon milk jugs filled with water. When it was hot, they put a table fan in their fireplace with a frozen jug of water in front and let the cool air blow.

I finally got the concept down and talked to one of my school parents who was a building contractor about how to do it. After I showed him the plans I had carefully drawn on draft paper, including elevations, Mr. Frye thought for a few minutes and studied my presentation. He joked, "This is going to look funny from the street."

He then looked at me seriously and said, "So, you want me to build you a basement with a roof on it with wide overhangs. And, you want to have sliding doors all along the south wall—is that about right?" I was shocked as I absorbed his perfect summation of what we wanted for a home. He suggested that on a gently sloping lot that we would need to be a bit creative with excavation and lot slope, that we would need to treat the structure like a basement with waterproofing and corrugated pipe to drain excess water. He also suggested increasing the "R-value" by layering the home envelope.

After the footing and reinforced concrete slab was poured and set and the drain piping buried in sand the walls started going up. The interior portion of the envelope was 8" concrete cinder blocks. Outside the blocks a veneer of common clay brick was laid with an air gap of about one inch between. Next, the concrete blocks were filled with granular Perlite ® insulation. Once the roof was on and before the interior was completed the wall was covered with one inch thick foam board insulation which gave us a 14" thick wall which was then sealed with wood paneling, a décor statement of the 80's.

The slight slope of the lot from north to south allowed for about four feet of excavation. The removed dirt was sloped on the west, north, and east sides towards the house so that on those side the berm reached to a level of 5 feet above the floor level.

On the south side, two sets of 8' wide sliding doors opened the interior to sunshine in the winter that reached up to 17' inside the home, heating the floor for nighttime release. In the summer months the high-in-the-sky sun did not penetrate into the home and we were rarely uncomfortable with no air-conditioning.

There were lots of jokes from family and friends about our hobbit, smurf, and troll sized home. Traffic would slow and people would stare. We, however, were very happy with our home and that electric bill went from hundreds of dollars to less than $20.00 per month. It was a wonderful experience, and only a move to California in 1988 could have ever torn us away from that fantastic hybrid home in North Carolina.

EARTH BERMED TO 5' HIGH ON NORTH SIDE OF HOME. NO WINDOWS HERE.

EARTH BERM LEADS SLOWLY FROM STREET TO JUST UNER 2' DUALPANE WINDOWS ON WEST SIDE. HOME IS 5' UNDER GROUND AT THIS POINT AS WELL.

EARTH-BERMED, PASSIVE SOLAR HOME, EST. 1982

4227 BIG OAK CHURCH ROAD, EAGLE SPRINGS, N. C.

Ben Thomas

21: Into Deeper Shades of Green

Excuses, excuses, you hear them everyday. This little ditty is a summation of the next period in my life. Personal and family trauma, a 3000 mile move across the country, being out of work for a time, and failures to find balance in life all took me into a much lighter shade of green. This time there was no garden, no farm animals, and the scorching heat of the San Joaquin Valley of California.

We still were able to recycle, and we wasted nothing. We found a place in a sunny corner to plant some tomato and Zucunni plants. My wife used a clothes line to dry our clothes and washed dishes by hand. Our sons had to rotate on dish-washing and clothes line duties. Outgrown and older clothing and any other discarded items were donated to charity and we always gave to charities on a monthly basis.

Being poor again did not make us greener. It made it difficult to be green because of a limited budget. In fact, for a few years I did not even think about being eco-conscious at all. In retrospect, I have sympathy for those among us who are limited by circumstances. You can still be green. Someone should have reminded me of these and other ways to be a darker green even if you are poor:

♦ A reusable shopping bag or two

♦ Use as many CFLs as possible — when a light burns out go green

♦ Recycle aluminum, plastic, paper — you can even make money doing this

♦ Reduce your carbon footprint by using less throw away items

♦ Find as many ways as possible to live a greener life

I had not been through such a period of defeat as what I faced in the late '80s and early '90s. The bottom dropped out of my confidence and had it not been for the support of family and friends. The environment was the last thing on my mind. My wife, as always stepped up and took the leadership while I wallowed in self-pity and resentment towards the unfairness of life.

Around the world it's known as the golden rule . It IS a part of being environmentally conscious—in tune with the world around us. In Christian circles it is another one of those things that God tells us to do— "Bear one another's burdens" (Galatians 6:2) My deepest gratitude to my closest friends from First Assembly of God in Bakersfield, California who nurtured my family through trials and my wife's unexpected heart surgery. They not only practiced the golden rule, but the "Platinum Rule" as well: "Do unto others as they would have you do unto them." You can accomplish a lot with the support of friends.

I earned my real estate license in 1991 and started working part-time . I had found my niche again and my moxie was back by the grace of God. I remember worked up the real estate ladder until I had my broker's license and opened my on office with 5 agents, quickly expanding to a staff of over 70. With an unmatched marketing and image building campaign we were successful. However, it seemed that with waiting lists for new homes and bidding wars for re-sales that even in triple digit summer heat people were not that interested in being green. Only one builder even included solar panels as an option.

At that time Bakersfield, California was the fastest growing city in America and farm land was being eaten up by the 100's of acres for housing, commercial and industrial development, and schools and parks. It was exciting, but no one was thinking of the environment.

In 2005 my business partner had the brilliant idea to build high rise condos in a town that had only grown out, never up. His job was to raise the money while I worked to get the project developed and approved. I joined the International Council of Shopping Centers (ICSC) and began to learn from architects, real estate lawyers and the leadership of Cal State Bakersfield who's land we were to lease for the project. We had responded successfully to a Request for Proposals (RFP) for a project on the south side of campus.

One of my first decisions as project leader was to avoid fights with the city and organizations such as the Sierra Club. I did my research and insisted that the project be LEED Certified. I went personally and individually to each city council member, county supervisor, the mayor and city manager, state and national representatives and senators in our area and was excited to gain their support and encouragement. I also spent an afternoon with members of the Sierra Club to gain input on how they felt we could be "green." They admitted that no one had ever come to them before announcing plans for a large project. LEED, Solar Power, Water saving solutions, use of native plants and natural light. I was getting back in the environmental groove. The project was "approved" by the CSU Chancellor's office and Board of Trustees in January of 2007.

The reactions to my presentation of our LEED certified proposal was extremely diversified. First, there is skepticism and doubt. Then there were those who had to wait and check with their developer friends who might be made to look bad if a young upstart company developed something on such a large scale.

I will always be appreciative for Democratic State Representative and later, Senator Michael Rubio, who applauded our efforts and went on to push hard for environmental legislation while in Sacramento. (So sorry he is out of politics.) His republican counterpart listened to me patiently and thoughtfully. When I finished the presentation we stood up and walked around the desk to shake my hand. He told me that he enjoyed the presentation, wished us good luck, and than said "You know, this type project is just not a part of our party's agenda." Thanks Roy!

One thing that I did observe while I was successful in real estate was that the upper class seem to care less for the environment than the poor. It is the middle class that is doing all the work and that share the most concern for the environment. The most financially blessed among us seem to think that as long as they can afford to pay for huge cars and SUVs, as long as they can afford to heat and cool home of 3,000 to 5,000 square feet or more that they are exempt from any environmental consciousness.

That is a trait of the liberal left as well as the conservative right wings of our political spectrum. Maybe they will purchase some carbon offsets to balance the scales of their guilty conscious. More than likely they will just applaud environmental speakers, go to fancy dinners that have more waste than the Los Angeles landfill, and talk about the importance of being "green." The hypocrisy of the Entertainment industry is one of the saddest stories in America today.

I resigned from the real estate company in August of 2006 and agreed to continue to work of the mixed use project until it was approved. This approval came in January of 2007. Unfortunately the funding for the project failed, in part due to the changing financial situation and the bank and lending crisis.

Later in 2007 I found myself in coastal Ventura County. Good things usually come out of bad if you keep your head up and hold on the anchors in your life. I needed a new start and was still excited about the LEED project that wasn't going to happen. I also needed a niche in order to be successful in a new market area.

It was then that I earned my Eco-Broker's designation. EcoBroker is the premier green designation for real estate professionals. I made my mission one of "Helping clients to make energy saving, environmentally sustainable, and economically sound choices when buying or selling a home. My vision was to "help clients to make sustainable choices about where and how they live."

After leaving real estate , I opted to earn two additional designations as possible jobs or career choices. First I became certified by Green Irene to do home energy assessments. Green Irene was designed to lead families and small business owners to liv e healthier, safer and more sustainable lifestyles at home and at work.

In addition the audit report would provide them the opportunity to save money, energy and water by implementing the consulting service report and the green home and office products.

Next I earned my Building Performance Institute certification. The Building Performance Institute, Inc. (BPI) is the nation's premier standards development and credentialing organization for residential energy efficiency retrofit work. Becoming a certified energy auditor, performing blower door, gas leak, and other critical audit checklist items on homes seemed a great way to understand more about the "real" environmental movement at a grass roots level.

My motivation for the BPI and Green Irene Certifications was my changed website. As an Eco-Broker seeking to enable clients to use "green marketing" to sell their homes, I had many requests for assistance in locating energy efficient products and contractors to help clients green their homes. As a value-added service I had begun to add pages to my website to inform people about these local green business-es and contractors.

In March of 2008, I changed my website to www.YourEcoTeam.com, a non-real estate site that I thought would make a fun hobby. The site had under 30,000 hits in 2008, but by 2011 had over 200,000 hits and in 2012 just under 900,000 hits. The site also grew from 6 value-added pages to a real estate website with a few dozen links to over 40 pages with nearly 3000 links.

Our plans for 2014 are to have a new site up and running. It will be a socially interactive and searchable site that we intend to be in a YELP meets Angie's List format. The mission of the new website, www.EarthKnot.org will be "Helping accountable 'green' product, services, art and entertainment providers to connect with environmentally conscious consumers via socially engaging technologies." We have the concept and are currently working on a business plan, finding investors and forming relationships with environmentally conscious supporters. The opportunity is here, there is a need for this type web site and we are on the way.

It seems that in a very positive way I have been able to come full circle in my life back into a deeper shade of green. When I was a child I lived sustainably because we were poor and had not choice. As a young adult my wife and I were almost what one could call "evangelical hippies" as we maintained an organic lifestyle and built a passive solar home. Now I consider myself a green advocate and am actively engaged in promoting sustainability to the highest degree possible.

Ben Thomas

22: Sustainable Me

What should we agree upon in this nation of liberals and conservatives, Democrats and Republicans, Christians, Muslims, Hindus, Buddhists, Jews, Agnostics, Atheists, and members of every clan and tribe? What can bring us together to care for the earth, the supporter of all life?

I have my evangelical Christian beliefs, my way to heaven, my faith in one Jehovah God and the atoning work of His only be-gotten son, Jesus Christ. I'm sure even the most diametrically op-posed person can be respectful enough to allow me that choice. And whatever your belief may be (although I wish you would con-sider mine), I will respect and defend your right to believe as you do. This is the United States of America.

You believe in climate change and global warming—I'm not completely convinced in that science yet. But I want to listen and learn and meanwhile do MY part to care for the earth. Take those two issues out of the discussion for a moment and let's assume for the sake of argument that there is no global warming or climate change. Would you be less passionate about the environment? I hope not.

If you've ever walked a path through the woods or by the ocean's shore— seen a wild animal running free — listened to a bird or insect on the wing — how could you not hear nature say, "save me, I am yours to enjoy."

On the other hand, if science is right, how can that possibly be a reason for anyone who doubts a scientific conclusion to treat the environment with any less care and concern? As discussed in this book, every major religion in the world has as a part of its belief that we should be responsible for the protection and care of the environment.

As a challenge to evangelical Christians and conservatives, let me share with you some Scripture that the Bible refers to as signs of the coming of the end of the age. To you who do not believe and think this is all mumbo-jumbo, please read these few words. You will have to agree with these projections made thousands of years ago:

♦ Daniel 12:4 "But you Daniel, shut up the words and seal the book until the time of the end; many shall run to and fro ,and knowledge shall increase."

♦ Matthew 24:7 "For nation will rise against nation, and kingdom against kingdom. And there will be famines, pestilences, and earthquakes in various places."

♦ Luke 21:25-26 "And there will be signs in the sun, in the moon, and in the stars; and on the earth distress of nations, with perplexity, the sea and the waves roaring; men's hearts failing them from fear and the expectation of those things which are coming on the earth, for the powers of the heavens will be shaken."

I'm sure that Christians are thinking, "yeah, um-huh, I told you so." Well, "yeah, I think you ought to read it again." It sure sounds like Matthew and Luke were talking about climate change and global warming — I'm just saying. You can't just believe the parts you want folks and deny the rest.

I know it just gets under your skin — no matter what you believe— that you have some beliefs and intentions that you share with those who are not of your persuasion. I have six words for all of you: "Build a bridge, get over it."

We all believe that the earth will keep rotating on its axis and that there will be a tomorrow. We believe that man needs nourishment to stay alive. We can see that pollution is getting worse and worse around the world. We believe that peace is the best choice.

Being "eco-conscious" means being aware of what you are doing, buying, using, and what it does to the environment. You can find many ways to help save our environment by becoming involved with many environmental causes and green organizations. These groups also will provide many ways and opportunities to help keep our world safe and ecologically sound. Become informed and active.

Please consider following the wisdom of my chosen "life verse" from I Peter 3:15: "Be ready to speak up and tell anyone who asks why you're living the way you are, and always with the utmost courtesy."

ABOUT THE AUTHOR

Ben Thomas

My journey is an interesting one. Growing up in rural North Carolina I saw life from a different perspective: Raised by parents who taught me to respect the environment and to live a sustainable lifestyle. We lived on a small organic farm where we grew our own food, preserved it after harvest, and shared its bounty with friends and neighbors.

In 1982, while looking for house plan ideas, I saw a magazine with articles on passive solar heating and earth-bermed houses. I remember the contractor saying to me, "So, you want me to build a basement with a roof on it and a glass wall all along the south side, right?" Several months later the environmentally sustainable, energy efficient home was built in central North Carolina.

In March, 2008 I segued my real estate website with its value-added "green" pages into YourEcoTeam.com, a "Yellow Pages for Green Stuff" site which will become *EarthKnot.org* in 2014, a search-able, socially interactive site to connect sustainable businesses with environmentally conscious consumers.

In fall of 2013, I released my first environmental book titled "Sustainable Me: Green Tips and Terms for the Environmentally Conscious." My first effort included an extensive Green Glossary of green terms, a list of environmental charities, as well as an eco-reading list of periodicals and books.

Regardless of your background, the environmental 'tent' is large enough to encompass every diversity the world has to offer in our quest to protect the earth and its resources; and we must look past cultural, political and religious differences to the task at hand.

BS Education, MS in School Administration, Eco-Broker Certified Affiliate, Certified Building Professional Institute (BPI) Energy Auditor, National Green Business Bureau Platinum Certified
Developed YourEcoTeam.com Website as Hobby,
Personally Vetting over 3000 "Green" Web Links

Under Development is EarthKnot.org, a Socially Interactive, and Searchable Web Site for the Purpose of
"Connecting Sustainable Businesses with Environmentally Conscious Consumers"

www.ingramcontent.com/pod-product-compliance
Lightning Source LLC
Chambersburg PA
CBHW020509290526
45786CB00002B/538